Some theological technician   e apart but not how to put it back together, much less put it back to work. Adam Johnson has the know-how for reassembly. This Snapshot has a lot less Aulén and a lot more Jonathan Edwards than we've become accustomed to in books on the atonement. By putting it against the background of God's orchestrating attribute of wisdom, Johnson joins the irreducible complexity of atonement to the unsurpassable perfection of God. A worthy goal, worthily carried out.

—Fred Sanders, author of *The Deep Things of God* and coauthor of *Locating Atonement*

I know of no other theologian who has given themselves so fully to the doctrine of atonement, and I know of no other work that so helpfully introduces a constructive account for the church. Christ's atonement truly is a work "by, of, and for wisdom." Let Adam introduce you to Christ's work anew and show you how Christ reveals the wisdom of God.

—Kyle Strobel, author of *Formed for the Glory of God* and coauthor of *Beloved Dust*

Many books explore the cross of Christ in view of the mercy and justice of God. Adam Johnson changes the lens with this concise and clearly written book, offering a picture of Jesus' saving work as the culmination of the same divine wisdom through which all things were created. Divine wisdom is not a rival attribute to justice and mercy, but that quality that enables God to be fully himself in finding the fitting solution that achieves all God's purposes for a world fallen into folly. Johnson has written a helpful book that brings fresh air into well-trod doctrinal paths, to which grateful readers can only respond, "And behold, it was very good"!

—Kevin J. Vanhoozer, author of *Is There a Meaning in this Text?* and *The Drama of Doctrine*

Taking his cue from Jonathan Edwards's sermon series, "The Wisdom of God in the Way of Salvation," Adam Johnson offers a short, clear, and accessible account of the work of Christ in atonement as the outworking of divine wisdom. The result is a terrific introduction to the doctrine of the atonement, from which students and their teachers are sure to profit.

—Oliver D. Crisp, coauthor of *Locating Atonement*

THE RECONCILING
WISDOM OF GOD

REFRAMING THE DOCTRINE OF THE ATONEMENT

Also in the Snapshots series:

Transformation: The Heart of Paul's Gospel
by David A. deSilva

Heirs of Promise: The Church as the New Israel in Romans
by P. Chase Sears

For updates on this series, visit LexhamPress.com

THE RECONCILING WISDOM OF GOD

REFRAMING THE DOCTRINE OF THE ATONEMENT

Snapshots

Michael F. Bird, Series Editor

Adam J. Johnson

LEXHAM PRESS

The Reconciling Wisdom of God: Reframing the Doctrine of the Atonement
Snapshots

Copyright 2016 Adam J. Johnson

Lexham Press, 1313 Commercial St., Bellingham, WA 98225
LexhamPress.com

Print ISBN 9781577997252
Digital ISBN 9781577997269

Series Editor: Michael F. Bird
Lexham Editorial: Elliot Ritzema, Abigail Stocker, Joel Wilcox
Cover Design: Jim LePage
Back Cover Design: Liz Donovan
Typesetting: ProjectLuz.com

Father, Son and Holy Spirit,
grant a double share of your wisdom
to my three sons,
Reuben, Nathan, and Simeon,
to whom I dedicate this book.

TABLE OF CONTENTS

ACKNOWLEDGMENTS

This short book on wisdom has progressed through a variety of stages. A number of friends, mentors, and publishers lie in its wake, deserving their respective tips of the hat.

The earliest version was a research paper for Prof. Sang Lee at Princeton Theological Seminary, and I thank both him and Prof. Daniel Migliore for their encouragement in this project.

Subsequently, this topic took shape as a paper presented at the Los Angeles Theology Conference in 2015, co-written with Kyle Strobel. It was later published as part of the conference proceedings in *Locating Atonement: Explorations in Constructive Dogmatics*. I would like to thank Kyle for this great experience, as well as Katya Covrett, Oliver Crisp, and Fred Sanders for their help and encouragement, and for the excellent conference they have developed over the last few years.

A research fellowship at Biola University's Center for Christian Thought (CCT), made possible through the support of a grant from the John Templeton Foundation, provided me with the time to write this book. While the opinions expressed in this publication are my own and do not necessarily reflect the views of the John Templeton Foundation or the CCT, I benefited greatly from the friendship, insight, and questions of the other fellows. I am particularly grateful for the leadership provided by Tom Crisp, Gregg Ten Elshof, and Steve Porter within the CCT, and from the friendship and help of Evan Rosa, the CCT assistant director. Laura Smit provided some exceptionally helpful recommendations and sources, and Kent Dunnington helped me appreciate the ways that the metaphysical and theological commitments of our religious commitments shape our understandings of different intellectual virtues.

Brannon Ellis, the acquisitions editor at Lexham Press, was the one who originally approached me about writing a short, yet (hopefully) creative, introductory text on the doctrine of the atonement, and then oversaw the editing and publishing of this book. Without his instigation and encouragement, I would not have embarked on this project.

As usual, a number of friends and students contributed in various ways to this project. I would like to think Glen and Susie Johnson, Scott Harrower, Matt Jenson, Ryan Peterson, Fred Sanders, Ben Sutton, and Jeremy Treat. Yet again Rachael Smith, my research assistant, was beyond helpful in a number of ways for this project. The broader community and culture within Biola University and the Torrey Honors Institute continues to push, encourage, and stimulate me. A greater contribution still lies with my wife, Katrina, and our sons, Reuben, Nathan, and Simeon: thank you for the balance and joy you bring to my life, which in turn gives me energy and joy for my work as a teacher and theologian.

And while this may be a little unusual, I would be utterly remiss if I did not express my profound thanks to Jonathan Edwards, whose set of sermons entitled "The Wisdom of God in the Way of Salvation" unlocked for me the doctrine of the atonement. I cannot imagine how my view of Christ's saving work would look today were it not for his preaching—my debt of gratitude is insurmountable.

On Telling Stories

There are any number of ways to tell a good story. It can begin with scenes of everyday life and gradually swell to epic proportions, as in Tolkien's *Lord of the Rings*. It can begin in the middle before looking back for context, as in Homer's *Odyssey*. It can focus on a single individual or, like Hugo's *Les Misérables*, weave together the lives of countless characters and families. Each has its limitations, and each has its way of gripping us—pulling us in so that we find ourselves caught up in the movement and action. There is no one right way to do it.

The doctrine of the atonement, no less than the Battle of Gettysburg or the *Adventures of Tom Sawyer*, is a matter of telling a story, or retelling God's story. One can do it any number of ways. At its heart, the atonement is a story, a history; and as with all stories, this telling is an art. The purpose of this book is to retell the story of Christ's atonement in a way that energizes future tellings in ever new and faithful ways.[1] And to

---

1. Cf. Stephen Sykes, *The Story of Atonement* (London: Darton, Longman, and Todd, 1997).

do this, we will not begin at the beginning—not in Jerusalem with the death and resurrection of Jesus—but in Sweden in 1930.

Aulén's Tale and Its Legacy

Gustaf Aulén, a Swedish theologian, sought to move past the division he perceived between the rationalistic Lutheran orthodoxy and the liberal theology of his day. To do so, he developed a historical and theological account of the atonement, positing three major periods in the history of the church.[2] In the first millennium (and in the writings of Martin Luther), theologians saw Christ's work in terms of overcoming Satan's power (what Aulén called the "classic" theory). Building on a number of passages throughout the Bible, this view emphasizes the role of Satan in God's fallen creation (Eph 2:2), the power he has over us (1 John 5:19), and the ways in which Christ came to defeat Satan, reestablishing us as the servants of God (Heb 2:14–15).[3]

The next half millennium or more was dominated by versions of the satisfaction theory (developed by Anselm of Canterbury), in which Christ in some way satisfies the honor or justice of God through his death. This theory prioritizes the relationship between God and humankind, emphasizing that which we owed to God yet could not pay, whether that be honor, justice, or otherwise. The burden of the argument falls

---

2. Gustaf Aulén, *Christus Victor: An Historical Study of the Three Main Types of the Idea of Atonement*, trans. A. G. Hebert (New York: Macmillan, 1951). Cf. Roland Spjuth, "Gustaf Aulén," in *Bloomsbury Companion to the Atonement*, ed. Adam J. Johnson (New York: Bloomsbury, forthcoming).

3. For recent work on this family of approaches, see Nicholas E. Lombardo, *The Father's Will: Christ's Crucifixion and the Goodness of God* (New York: Oxford, 2013), 181–239; Adam Johnson, *Atonement: A Guide for the Perplexed* (New York: T&T Clark, 2015), 166–71.

on the way or ways in which Jesus Christ restores to God that which we owe, that in him we might be restored to right relations with God. Penal substitution is a version of this theory, wherein Jesus satisfied God by enduring the punishment we ought to have suffered for our sin.

The third period owed much to Peter Abelard's exemplarist or "subjective" theory, in which Christ's death transforms us through its inspiring example. Abelard's thought has been significantly reinterpreted in the last several decades, but this theory remains one of the most influential interpretations of the work of Christ, drawing our attention to the role of Christ's life in our salvation. While few (if any) theologians would deny this aspect of Christ's ministry, some (particularly during the Enlightenment and beyond) have made it the central or sole aspect of Christ's work.

Going beyond this historical account, Aulén argued that we should return to the original or "classic" theory of Christ's defeat of Satan, avoiding the later, perverted versions of the doctrine. Aulén's story caught the imagination of the church, and has proved to be of enduring value. Due in large part to Aulén's influence, the defeat of Satan as one of the primary aspects of the work of Christ is now a staple feature of any work on the atonement, and is one of the storylines that receives the most creative energy from theologians of the atonement today. But Aulén's telling of the story has its weaknesses, and unfortunately these have proved to be quite significant, precisely because his story was so compelling.[4]

---

4. I provide the details for this critique in chapter 1 of *Atonement: A Guide for the Perplexed*. Aulén's heritage is evident in a number of important texts, such as Robert Sherman, *King, Priest and Prophet: A Trinitarian Theology of Atonement* (New York: T&T Clark, 2004); Thomas F. Torrance, *Atonement: The Person and Work of Christ* (Downers Grove, IL: InterVarsity Press, 2009); Colin E. Gunton,

One weakness of Aulén's argument is his division of the history of the doctrine of the atonement into three different periods that focused on three different accounts of the work of Christ. The drama of this rendition of the doctrine is unquestionable. Much like a princess captured by two villains, the savior rescues the princess, bringing us back to the golden age before things went wrong. But a closer look reveals that while this may be compelling storytelling, there never were three such periods in the history of the church. Theologians of every age have held to all three of these aspects of the story (and a good deal more than three, in fact). Athanasius, Anselm, Thomas, Luther, Calvin, Edwards—all of these theologians from different eras of the church affirmed all three theories delineated by Aulén and a number of others besides. The closer we look into the history of theology, the more inadequate we find Aulén's thesis to be.

Second, the idea that one of these aspects or eras should have preeminence is equally faulty, because all are valid elements of Christ's work as attested in Scripture. To pit Scripture against Scripture in an attempt to solve the squabbles of rival theories is a doomed enterprise. To fight for free will by disregarding passages on predestination, to devote yourself to accumulating wealth by alienating all your family

---

The Actuality of Atonement: A Study of Metaphor, Rationality, and the Christian Tradition (Grand Rapids: Eerdmans, 1989). It is equally influential in related disciplines, such as philosophical or analytic theology. Cf. the basic structure in the argument of Gordon Graham, "Atonement," in *The Cambridge Companion to Christian Philosophical Theology*, ed. Charles Taliaferro and Chad V. Meister (New York: Cambridge University Press, 2010). The movement away from this heritage is manifest in a number of contemporary works, including Scot McKnight, *A Community Called Atonement* (Nashville: Abingdon, 2007); Mark D. Baker and Joel B. Green, *Recovering the Scandal of the Cross: Atonement in New Testament and Contemporary Contexts* (Downers Grove, IL: InterVarsity Press, 2003); Joel B. Green, "Kaleidoscopic View," in *The Nature of the Atonement: Four Views*, ed. James K. Beilby and Paul R. Eddy (Downers Grove, IL: IVP Academic, 2006).

and friends, or to fight for a ransom theory by disregarding or minimizing passages about propitiation simply will not do. To win is to lose what you were fighting for. If the Bible is the authoritative basis for the story we tell, we must be faithful to the whole of Scripture, refusing to break it up into supposedly competing subplots among which we may or must choose a favorite.[5] And as it turns out, Scripture is exceptionally reluctant to crown one of these accounts as preeminent over the others. Just as a groom dares not answer the question whether his bride is more beautiful, wise, or loving—or even limit her virtues to these three—we dare not prioritize or subjugate Scripture over Scripture.[6]

Finally, while it was dramatic, the story as Aulén told it left out important knights and princes, villains, kingdoms, and whole epochs. The doctrine of the atonement throughout Scripture and the history of doctrine is far richer, far more complex and delightful than this simplistic story of a princess and two villains would suggest. While such an abridged story may suffice for bedtime, a far greater and more complex story is necessary to do justice to the drama in which we find ourselves. While the adventures of Tom Sawyer are endearing, it is the story of Huckleberry Finn, set against the backdrop of slavery in the South, that is more compelling and transforming.

The good news is that the doctrine of the atonement, much like Lady Philosophy in Boethius' classic *Consolation of Philosophy*, lives still in all her undiminished vigor. The splendor of her clothes, however, is "obscured by a kind of film

---

5. After all, it is *all* of the Scriptures that "are able to make [us] wise for salvation through faith in Christ Jesus" (2 Tim 3:15).

6. There is, however, such a thing as weight or priority among passages of Scripture. Not all verses are equal, and neither are all themes or teachings.

as of long neglect," and her dress is "torn by the hands of marauders who had each carried off such pieces as he could get."[7] The problem is not so much with the doctrine itself as it is with the paltry mindset we have brought on ourselves by listening to distorted and inadequate stories. Stronger medicine is needed: a better, truer, and more faithful story. And for this story we turn to Lady Wisdom, because telling the story of Christ's work from the standpoint of divine wisdom offers us the best and fullest standpoint from which to appreciate the full height, depth, and breadth of this vast, masterful, and saving story of God's work for us and for our salvation (Eph 3:18).[8]

What we need is a standpoint from which to view the whole scene. This doesn't mean that it is the best standpoint in an unqualified, objective sense. Only God can simultaneously appreciate every aspect and dimension of the saving work of

---

7. Boethius, *The Consolation of Philosophy*, trans. V. E. Watts (New York: Penguin, 1999), 4.

8. I first explored this thesis in Adam Johnson and Kyle Strobel, "Atoning Wisdom: The Wisdom of God in the Way of Salvation," in *Locating Atonement*, ed. Oliver Crisp and Fred Sanders (Grand Rapids: Zondervan, 2015). The present work is a development and expansion of certain themes in that chapter, along with a more complete backstory to the project. It is worth noting that by *wisdom* I primarily mean *practical* wisdom, or *prudentia*. That said, there is no division between theoretical and practical wisdom within the life of God, both due to divine simplicity and because in the incarnation wisdom made itself practical. On the distinction between theoretical and practical wisdom, see W. Jay Wood, "Prudence," in *Virtues and Their Vices*, ed. Kevin Timpe and Craig A. Boyd (New York: Oxford University Press, 2014), 40. From a theological perspective, Barth writes that "the concept of knowledge, of *scientia*, is insufficient to describe what Christian knowledge is. We must rather go back to what in the Old Testament is called wisdom, what the Greeks called *sophia* and the Latins *sapientia*, in order to grasp the knowledge of theology in its fullness. *Sapientia* is distinguished from the narrower concept of *scientia*, wisdom is distinguished from knowing, in that it not only contains knowledge in itself, but also that this concept speaks of a knowledge which is practical knowledge, embracing the entire existence of man. Wisdom is the knowledge by which we may actually and practically live." Karl Barth, *Dogmatics in Outline*, trans. G. T. Thompson (New York: Harper, 1959), 25.

Christ. But given our finite and limited grasp of this story—this event—the perspective from which we view it matters greatly. A watchtower may be the best point from which to survey a valley or keep an eye out for forest fires, but is a poor place from which to fish.

Other approaches to retelling the story of Christ's work are best for other purposes, and I do not mean to give wisdom absolute pride of place as a king among princes or a lady among her attendants. To understand the racking guilt of a stricken conscience or the consuming and alienating shame of a stained soul, for instance, we would do best to move in other directions; these have more to do with justice (and guilt) than they do with wisdom (and folly). But under the present circumstances, the gravest danger we face is that of clinging to truths without appreciating the larger context in which they play their role. Nothing is quite so helpful for this as gaining the higher ground of wisdom to observe the lay of the land before us. Again, by "higher ground" I do not mean to suggest that wisdom holds a privileged position. The hills and the valleys both have their roles to play: the hill affords perspective, while the valley yields fertile soil for farming. (Let not the eye say to the foot: "I don't need you," or "I am better or more important than you!") Before attending directly to the role of wisdom in the atonement, however, I will briefly consider some of the basic elements of the doctrine.

The Structure of the Atonement

As with any story, the doctrine of the atonement has certain key elements that must be in place for the drama to emerge clearly, and for the portrayal of the resolution to be deep and compelling. In this case, given the scope of realities entailed

in the work of Christ, it is vitally important to have a sufficiently large structure or framework from which to tell the
story.[9] Starting with a princess and two villains simply won't
do. We need the full picture, and this picture begins with the
primary character in the story: the triune God. The reason for
this is that in this case, the main character and the history as
a whole are bound together. God is simultaneously the central
actor, the source of the setting and every other character, the
one around whom the whole drama revolves, and ultimately
the one in and through whom the whole drama is resolved.
This is no mere matter of a knight rescuing the princess. God
is far more bound up with every element of the plot, setting,
and cast than such an image would suggest, and sustained
attention to him at every level of the story guides us to a full
grasp of the whole.

God is the source of every other element of the story.
He sets the stage. His creatures are sustained by him, receive
their identity and purpose from him, sin against him, and
ultimately find themselves entirely within the sphere of his
intention, activity, and providence for their being and salvation. We must begin by asking: Who is this Creator God?
Why has he done what he has done? How does he respond to
our actions, whether sinful or otherwise? This is the bedrock;
this is the plumb line against which everything is measured
and everything is understood. If God is just, righteous, and
holy, then the ensuing story is cast in a certain light. If God is
loving, merciful, compassionate, and gracious, an altogether
different hue colors the scene. And if he is powerful, wise,

---

9. Similarly, David Ford speaks of doctrine as a "finely balanced ecology: a major
change in one niche is likely to have effects throughout" (David Ford, *Theology:
A Very Short Introduction* [New York: Oxford University Press, 2000], 105).

and all-knowing, yet another shade pervades every element of the story. These subtly alter it yet again, just as the score of a movie can fill the same scene with passion, fear, or calm.

But of course God is all these things and more. Augustine, in one of the most beautiful passages of one of his most beautiful books, writes:

> Most high, utterly good, utterly powerful, most omnipotent, most merciful and most just, deeply hidden yet most intimately present, perfection of both beauty and strength, stable and incomprehensible, immutable and yet changing all things ... always active, always in repose, gathering to yourself but not in need, supporting and filling and protecting, creating and nurturing and bringing to maturity, searching even though to you nothing is lacking: you love without burning, you are jealous in a way that is free of anxiety, you "repent" (Gen. 6:6) without pain of regret, you are wrathful and remain tranquil. You will a change without any change in your design. You recover what you find, yet have never lost. Never in any need, you rejoice in your gains (Luke 15:7); you are never avaricious, yet you require interest (Matt. 25:27). We pay you more than you require so as to make you our debtor, yet who has anything which does not belong to you? (1 Cor. 4:7). You pay off debts,

> though owing nothing to anyone; you cancel
> debts and incur no loss.[10]

God is the one who, in his "wonderful circle of divine simplicity," is everything that he is with completeness and consistency, without conflict or internal strife.[11] And he is ever enacting the divine life and character in himself as Father, Son, and Holy Spirit, showering that life out upon us through his activity in his creation and the story of salvation. Who is God? He is the ever-rich God who reveals his character through the life he lives with us as our God; the God who identified and named himself in the course of his history with Israel (the God of Abraham, Isaac, and Jacob), and then definitively through the incarnation; the Son of God made man through the will of the Father and in the power of the Holy Spirit.

Who is this God? We can only begin to describe him by telling the story of his work over and over again, reflecting now upon his love, then upon his freedom, and later upon his justice, weaving these together in the oneness of the divine life with yet other qualities of God's character. We describe

---

10. Augustine, *Confessions*, trans. Henry Chadwick (Oxford: Oxford University Press, 1991), 4–5.

11. Once more Lady Philosophy accompanies our story, as the "wonderful circle of divine simplicity" plays as pivotal a role here as it does in the restoration of Boethius (Boethius, *The Consolation of Philosophy*, 81). On the relation of atonement to divine simplicity, see Stephen R. Holmes, "A Simple Salvation? Soteriology and the Perfections of God," in *God of Salvation*, ed. Ivor J. Davidson and Murray A. Rae (Burlington, VT: Ashgate, 2011); Adam Johnson, *God's Being in Reconciliation: The Theological Basis of the Unity and Diversity of the Atonement in the Theology of Karl Barth* (New York: T&T Clark, 2012). Though he does not say as much, J. I. Packer makes a similar point in writing about the divine wisdom when he claims that "wisdom, as the old theologians used to say, is his *essence*, just as power, and truth, and goodness, are his *essence*—integral elements, that is, in his character" (J. I. Packer, *Knowing God* [Downers Grove, IL: InterVarsity Press, 1993], 90). The reason all these attributes are God's essence is that God is simple. Within his one and undivided essence is a plurality of attributes without division or conflict.

him as holy, wise, or longsuffering, stopping long enough to honor him as such, and then we move on lest we leave out other aspects of his character. God is who he is, and we know him as such, and speak of him as such, only as we witness to and in turn speak of who he has shown himself to be in the history of his action, preeminently in the work of Jesus Christ.[12]

But here we run up against a problem, because the telling of stories relies on omission. As John McPhee says:

> Writing is selection. Just to start a piece of writing you have to choose one word and only one from more than a million in the language. Now keep going. What is your next word? Your next sentence, paragraph, section, chapter? Your next ball of fact. You select what goes in and you decide what stays out.[13]

We craft stories by choosing which elements to highlight and which relevant factors to omit. Think, for instance, of how little we know of most characters that play even significant roles in a familiar story—this point was made delightfully in Tom Stoppard's *Rosencrantz and Guildenstern are Dead*, based on two minor characters from Shakespeare's *Hamlet*. Telling a story requires the careful selection of details and the omitting or abridging of a whole host of others. A story without omission and abridgement would not be a story—it would be reality,

---

12. As Gregory of Nyssa reminds us, "we must not attribute to [God] one transcendent attribute, and then exclude another which equally befits him. But our faith must certainly include every sublime and devout thought of God, and these must be properly related to each other." Gregory of Nyssa, "An Address on Religious Instruction," in *Christology of the Later Fathers*, ed. Edward R. Hardy (Philadelphia: Westminster, 1954), 301.

13. John McPhee, "Omission: Choosing What to Leave Out," *The New Yorker*, September 14, 2015, http://www.newyorker.com/magazine/2015/09/14/omission.

not as we experience it, but as experienced by an omniscient narrator. A story without omission would take even longer to tell than it took the event itself to happen, since the event itself is far more complex than any one person's experience of it. We tell stories by omitting a great deal of context, focusing on a handful of connected events, and then omitting a great number of related consequences or responses. Story is the art of abridging reality from a particular vantage point and for a particular purpose.

While this is clearly true of the life of Jesus (as is evident in the differences between the four Gospel accounts),[14] this is equally true in theological accounts of his death and resurrection. Every theory or account of Christ's atonement selects certain aspects by means of which to tell the story. In *Atonement: A Guide for the Perplexed*, I argue that the single most important factor in determining the vantage point from which the story of atonement is told is the divine attribute that is selected to define God's purposes, the character of our sin, and the nature of our salvation. More than any other factor, stories or theories of the atonement derive their uniqueness from the characteristic of God they use to shape the whole. Put differently, theories of the atonement are abridged explanations of the work of Christ that use one or a small group of divine attributes to determine which material to incorporate.

Penal substitution, for instance, emphasizes the justice of God, our guilt before him, and the justice and righteousness into which we are established and formed through the work of the risen Christ. Even though it includes the mercy and love of God, the primary features of this theory are shaped above

---

14. Think of the claim that Jesus did many other things that, if told, would fill all the books in the world (John 21:25).

all by justice; it is the glacier that carves out the defining crags and cliffs of this valley. Quite different but equally biblical accounts of Christ's work emerge when we retell the story in light of God's holiness—in which we unholy and unclean sinners are made clean and holy by Christ—or his patience, his grace, or some other attribute. Each telling is fully biblical. But just as Chaim Potok could have told his novel *The Chosen* from the perspectives of Reuven, Danny, either of their fathers, or an omniscient narrator, so one can develop the doctrine of the atonement from any number of equally valid, significant, and biblical accounts of the character of God.

Many theologians have implicitly or explicitly defended the notion of "key" attributes within the divine life. In sermons or theological discourse, one may emphasize the centrality of divine love and another divine justice, with profound implications for how they develop and organize their theological and ethical commitments. I take it as given in this book that God does not have a "master attribute" of which all the others are subservient parts or elements. God, who is simple and has no divisions or parts, is all that he is in all that he does without division or part. Though I do not defend this claim here, I believe it follows that there is no "master virtue"—no central virtue that includes within itself all other virtues.[15]

---

15. Against this, Roberts and Wood argue that "practical wisdom has a privileged place in the array of intellectual virtues, one that corresponds to the special place occupied by the love of knowledge. ... Both of these virtues pervade the intellectually excellent life, showing up as a presupposition or necessary background of all the other virtues." (Robert Campbell Roberts and W. Jay Wood, *Intellectual Virtues: An Essay in Regulative Epistemology* [New York: Oxford, 2007], 305). Plato makes a similar claim in the *Laws*, I.631. My response would involve an affirmation of this claim, complemented by similar claims of all the other virtues, rooted in the unity of the virtues and the simplicity of the divine life from which they stem. Implicit within this is an understanding of the virtues not merely as "helps for the present life" or "habits that prepare us for a deeper communion with God in the life to come," but as our creaturely participation in the excellences (or

In formulating theories of the atonement, we must work from the event of the incarnation, life, death, and resurrection of Jesus Christ, which is retold and witnessed to in any number of ways throughout Scripture. To be faithful to this event and these retellings, we too must learn the art of telling and retelling this story in ever new, yet faithful ways.

In this book, I will tell the story of the work of Christ from the standpoint of divine wisdom. As we will see, this standpoint more than any other opens our eyes to the full size and scope of the wondrous, epic story of the work of Jesus. More than any other, this account of the history of Jesus the Messiah of Israel gives us a sense of the whole doctrine; in turn it equips us to tell the story in ever new ways, from ever more perspectives, to the benefit and nourishment of the church.

This is not to say that wisdom is the "master attribute"— it remains one aspect of the single, simple character of God that allows for no parts, divisions, or conflict. But each attribute of God affords a different and unique insight into his character and his creation, and in this particular case I am arguing that the wisdom of God gives us a remarkable vantage point for appreciating the scope of God's (re)creative work in Christ.

What is at stake in how we tell the story of Jesus' death and resurrection? As we have seen, in every story certain events or aspects are highlighted and others omitted. But if we fail to attend to this, if we confuse the story for the event itself, then we run the risk of making our omissions permanent. If I recount my life through the vantage point of my relationship with my father, this is good and accurate, since my father had

attributes) proper to the divine life (Kevin Timpe and Craig A. Boyd, *Virtues and Their Vices* [New York: Oxford, 2014], 29).

an immense and wonderfully formative influence on my life. But if this is the only story I tell and the only way I think of my life, I run the risk of permanently omitting and forgetting so many riches! My mother, sister, countless friends and devoted teachers, coaches, pastors, and mentors leap to mind, not to mention the saving work of the triune God throughout my life. If we mistake our telling of the work of Christ for the thing itself, and if we (even unintentionally) make our omissions permanent and final, we run the risk of distorting and shrinking the gospel to the point that it fails to be a faithful representation of the saving work of Jesus Christ, God become man for us and for our salvation.

CHAPTER 1

Atonement as a Work of Wisdom: Snapshots from Scripture

At first, telling the story of the work of Christ from the standpoint of divine wisdom might seem obscure and probably unhelpful, rather like telling the story of Abraham Lincoln from the perspective of his best friend's gardener. After all, isn't the atonement primarily a matter of our disobedience, God's wrath, and his decision to turn toward us in grace and love? Isn't Christ's work that of a priestly sacrifice? And while the opposite of wisdom—folly—certainly isn't good, does it do justice to the full horror and depravity of our sin? Surely wisdom plays a role in all this, since God is wise, but does it have the weight, the force, to play the starring role?

It turns out that wisdom has been starring in this role all along. This angle is far more central to the way Scripture thinks about the cross than we otherwise might presume. We often get stuck in ruts or patterns of thinking, missing out on large portions and themes of Scripture if we are not careful. But the Bible has a great deal to say about the work of Christ being a work of wisdom. As Karl Barth puts it:

> There can be no doubt that in the New Testament Canon, as in that of the Old Testament, the wisdom teaching has become an integral part of the apostolic preaching. Paul would not be Paul without 1 Cor. 1–2, and the whole context of Colossians and Ephesians would disintegrate if for some reason it were desired to remove this stone from the edifice. Jesus Christ, our righteousness, sanctification and redemption, is also our wisdom, and faith in Him is our instruction by the wisdom of God.[1]

Taking Barth's lead, we can look to 1 Corinthians to launch us into this theme, with its dichotomy of human and divine wisdom:

> For since, in the wisdom of God, the world did not know God through wisdom, it pleased God through the folly of what we preach to save those who believe. For Jews demand signs and Greeks seek wisdom, but we preach Christ crucified, a stumbling block to Jews and folly to Gentiles, but to those who are called, both Jews and Greeks, Christ is the power of God and the wisdom of God (1 Cor 1:21–24).

What does this passage claim about how wisdom relates to Christ's work? First, it is an event "in the wisdom of God."

---

1. Karl Barth, *Church Dogmatics* II/1: *The Doctrine of God*, ed. G. W. Bromiley and T. F. Torrance (Edinburgh: T&T Clark, 1980), 439.

God is wise, and this work occurred in his wisdom. Affronting the wise of the earth, the wisdom of God stands forth in this act, revealing itself in Christ. The work of the cross, far from being an arbitrary, unfortunate, or unplanned-for tragedy, has the full backing of the wisdom of God; it occurred *in* his wisdom.

Second, this work of wisdom concerns not merely the teaching of Jesus, but Christ crucified.[2] While Christ was certainly a wisdom teacher, fulfilling the role of the teacher and sage (John 3:2) and bringing to life the Wisdom literature of the Old Testament, this is not the focus here.[3] Paul is concerned with the crucifixion of Christ, which occurred in God's wisdom. The *cross* was the wise act of the creator God.

Third, Christ himself is said to be "the power of God and the wisdom of God." Paul here weaves together the character of God, the work of Christ, and the person of Christ around the theme of divine wisdom. Within the larger context of 1 Corinthians 1, through the incorporation of the work of the Holy Spirit, Paul effectively makes a Trinitarian claim, weaving the person and work of Christ together with the work of the Father and the Spirit in such a way as to irrevocably establish the wisdom of this event. Wisdom thus brings together

---

2. Not all take this path, of course. Peter Hodgson takes the opposite approach, emphasizing the life and teaching Christ. Properly construed, of course, these are profoundly complementary. See Peter Crafts Hodgson, *God's Wisdom: Toward a Theology of Education* (Louisville: Westminster John Knox, 1999), 88.

3. Some have placed great emphasis on Jesus as the incarnate Wisdom of Proverbs, developing a wisdom Christology on those grounds. Our approach emphasizes Jesus as the wisdom of God, without making a claim regarding Lady Wisdom in Proverbs. Along those lines, I find Gathercole's point helpful: "Wisdom was, by and large, not regarded in Judaism as a preexistent *entity* distinct from or independent of God, but rather as an attribute of God and a way of speaking about his purpose: in short, a personification rather than a person" (Simon J. Gathercole, *The Preexistent Son: Recovering the Christologies of Matthew, Mark, and Luke* [Grand Rapids: Eerdmans, 2006], 209).

the work of the whole Trinity and the person and work of Christ, focusing on the cross and the empty tomb.

But what precisely establishes this as a work of wisdom? First Corinthians explores the choice, purpose, and power of God toward our salvation, employing wisdom as the aspect of God's character that brings these together in his work. Three times Paul writes that it "pleased God," and he writes that "God chose" (1 Cor 1:27-28) this path. Wisdom is a matter of the choice of God—of his good pleasure. Although, as Thomas Aquinas writes, God is pure act,[4] he is a God who deliberates, who makes choices, considers, and sets himself upon courses of action.[5] This means that God does not make decisions based on random choice or whim, because "with God are wisdom and might; he has counsel and understanding" (Job 12:13). The triune God is neither fickle nor capricious. This is a careful and purposive choice, deeply rooted in and harmonious with the divine character. It is ordered toward an end or goal that runs equally deep in the heart of God: "to save those who believe," and also to "shame the wise" and "to bring to nothing things that are." The wisdom of God is the choice of God; this choice is rooted in his being and character and is ordered toward a purpose that likewise stems from his being and character.

But God's wisdom consists of yet more, because while this choice is purposive and intentional, and therefore consistent

---

4. Thomas Aquinas, *Light of Faith: The Compendium of Theology* (Manchester, NH: Sophia Institute Press, 1993), 15.

5. Compare, for instance, the deliberation of God, as it is contrasted with the deliberation of humankind, in Gen 1:26; 11:3-4; and 11:7. On God's deliberation, Barth writes: "God is wise in so far as His whole activity, as willed by Him, is also thought out by Him, and thought out by Him from the very outset with correctness and completeness, so that it is an intelligent and to that extent a reliable and liberating activity." Barth, *Church Dogmatics* II/1, 425-26. On the human plane, Roberts and Wood describe wisdom as "a power of deliberation—of figuring out how to accomplish what is good" (Roberts and Wood, *Intellectual Virtues*, 310).

with the whole being and purpose of God, it is also combined with his power, and therefore it is meaningful and effective. As far removed from every sterile good intention as the night is from the day, as the east from the west, the wisdom of God stands between his will on the one hand and his power on the other. Wisdom is the integration of the two, and therefore the powerful enactment of his good pleasure to bring about his good purposes. Unlike the wisdom of the nations, this is no mere speculation. This wisdom is not limited to wise sayings, like the Calormenes and their many proverbs in C. S. Lewis' *The Horse and His Boy*, or abstract concepts that are theoretically good but utterly unachievable. The wisdom of God, because it is the wisdom of the God who is both good and powerful, is an active and effective wisdom. It brings about our salvation (1 Cor 1:18) and shames the wise, because this is the "only wise God" who deserves "glory forevermore through Jesus Christ" (Rom 16:27).

In Ephesians Paul takes us further still, expanding the scope of his vision from a conflict between the foolish and the wise of this world to a cosmic vista of the battle in the spiritual realms. There Paul tells us of God's "plan of the mystery hidden for ages": that "through the church the manifold wisdom of God might now be made known to the rulers and authorities in the heavenly places. This was according to the eternal purpose that he has realized in Christ Jesus our Lord" (Eph 3:9–11). But what is this manifold wisdom? And how is it related to the death and resurrection of Christ?

Once again we see that Christ's death and resurrection are works of wisdom. This is a matter of God's good choosing, of his purposing and reaching forward to a goal that is near to his heart, and in which he exercises his power so that his wisdom is effective. "Blessed be the God and Father of our Lord Jesus Christ, who has blessed us in Christ with every spiritual blessing in the heavenly places, even as he chose us in him before the foundation of the world" (Eph 1:3)! God chose us. This is God's wisdom—it is his choice. But this choice reaches forward "to the praise of his glorious grace" (Eph 1:6), and it is powerful, because he is the one "who works all things according to the counsel of his will," a counsel that does not stand on its own but is bound up with his powerful working. In his power, "the LORD brings the counsel of the nations to nothing; he frustrates the plans of the people." His counsel, on the other hand, "stands forever, the plans of his heart to all generations" (Psa 33:11), for in his power and wisdom he brings them to creation.

But this is no mere repetition of what we found in 1 Corinthians. Here we find that God's wisdom is a matter of mystery. While the wise of this world did not have access to the wisdom of God in 1 Corinthians, we now see that the wisdom of God is a hidden reality, a mystery unveiled only by the work of God as he makes known to us "the mystery of his will, according to his purpose" (Eph 1:9). This is a making-known that occurs only "by revelation" (Eph 3:3); as a choice of God, it is his good pleasure to share, to make known. The wisdom of God is not a necessity waiting to be grasped or a reality sitting on the surface of creation to be casually observed by every creature—it is a mystery made known only as a part of God's intentional work to reveal it.

But to say that this is the hidden good pleasure of God, revealed only at his will, could sound as though this were a contingent reality—as if God has not woven his purposes into the fabric of his creation. Is this true? Are these purposes mere decoration, or are they architectural, making their way down into the very structure of creation itself? Ephesians 1:4 is one of those few passages in Scripture that takes us back to creation, and then further back still: God "chose us in him *before the foundation of the world*." Later, Paul writes that it was given to him to preach:

> ... the plan of the mystery hidden for ages in God who created all things, so that through the church the manifold wisdom of God might now be made known to the rulers and authorities in the heavenly places. This was according to the *eternal purpose* that he has realized in Christ Jesus our Lord (Eph 3:9–11, emphasis added).

The purposes of God are hidden in God, but they are also God's eternal purposes; they are woven into the very structure of creation, and are no mere decoration. And the mystery, the goal and purpose, was that God, "in the fullness of time," would "unite all things in him, things in heaven and things on earth" (Eph 1:10)—a mystery that is essentially the telos and purpose of all creation. And how does he do this? Through Christ's resurrection from the dead (Eph 1:20), a claim Paul establishes at length elsewhere (1 Cor 15).

Thus the wisdom of God, in addition to being the effective choice of God that brings about his purposes, is a cosmic reality woven into the fabric of the universe for bringing about his good purposes through the death (Eph 2:13) and resurrection (Eph 1:20) of Jesus Christ. The wisdom of God is a work of the Father, Son, and Holy Spirit, established before the foundation of the world to bring about the reconciliation and union of all things through Christ's death and resurrection.

This is the trajectory we see concluded in Romans 11, where Paul celebrates the consigning of all to disobedience that God might have mercy on all, uniting Jew and Gentile: "Oh, the depth of the riches and wisdom and knowledge of God! How unsearchable are his judgments and how inscrutable his ways!" (Rom 11:33).[6] The wisdom of God, hidden but now revealed, was woven into the fabric of God's covenantal history with Israel and, as Paul's letter to the Ephesians shows, into the very fabric of creation. It is this wisdom of God that we celebrate in his bringing to completion and union all things in heaven and earth through the death and resurrection of his Son, Jesus Christ.

There is one further thing to note in this brief tour of the wisdom of God as seen in Scripture. God's purposes are cosmic in reach; the wisdom of God's reconciliation decisively affects every aspect of the cosmos. The wisdom of God in this plan brings about the reconciliation of *all things*.[7] The wisdom of God concerns all things in heaven and earth, since it was in and by wisdom that God created. The Lord possessed wisdom at the beginning of his work (Prov 11:22-31); it was in wisdom that he made his works, his creatures (Psa 104:24-26); and it was by his wisdom that he founded the world (Jer 10:12). And given the relation between Christ and wisdom

---

6. As John of the Cross puts it, "This thicket of God's wisdom and knowledge is so deep and immense that no matter how much the soul knows, she can always enter it further; it is vast and its riches incomprehensible, as St. Paul exclaims: *O height of the riches of the wisdom and knowledge of God, how incomprehensible are his judgments and unsearchable his ways* [Rom. 11:33]." John of the Cross, "The Spiritual Canticle," in *The Collected Works of St. John of the Cross* (Washington, DC: Institute of Carmelite Studies, 1979), 613. Subsequently, John writes that "a soul with an authentic desire for divine wisdom wants suffering first in order to enter this wisdom by the thicket of the cross" (ibid., 614).

7. Cf. Barth's expansive and even cosmic account of God's wisdom in Christ in *Church Dogmatics* II/1, 438-39.

established in 1 Corinthians 1:24 (where Christ is "the power of God and the wisdom of God"), this is precisely the logic we see unfolding in Colossians:

> He is the image of the invisible God, the first-born of all creation. For by him all things were created, in heaven and on earth, visible and invisible, whether thrones or dominions or rulers or authorities—all things were created through him and for him. And he is before all things, and in him all things hold together. And he is the head of the body, the church. He is the beginning, the firstborn from the dead, that in everything he might be preeminent. For in him all the fullness of God was pleased to dwell, and through him to reconcile to himself all things, whether on earth or in heaven, making peace by the blood of his cross (Col 1:15–20).

The connection between Jesus and wisdom is not explicit in this passage, but is clearly present in the broader context of Colossians and Ephesians. Here we see all the same dynamics in play: the preexistence of wisdom, the participation of wisdom in creation, and, most importantly for our purposes, wisdom as the means by which the reconciliation of all things is brought about.[8] For Paul, the wisdom of God is both the source of all things and the reconciliation of all things: the means by which God brings all things to peace and all things to rest in him. The work of wisdom is cosmic, both in scope and

---

8. This correlation is all the more likely given Paul's statement that in Christ "are hidden all the treasures of wisdom and knowledge" (Col 2:3), indicating not only a verbal but a conceptual link—Paul's writing about the union of creation, as well as reconciliation by the same agent, brought the theme of wisdom to his mind.

in the sense that it is the single means by which the creator God brings his creation to its fulfillment in himself. And at the heart of this work, the chosen means for its execution, is the death and resurrection of Jesus Christ—wisdom incarnate.[9]

We have seen from Scripture itself that there is every reason to explore the work of Christ as a work of wisdom. This is no mere tangent; it is a fully warranted way of telling the story of God and his history with his creation. The atonement is the enacted wisdom of God, the element of God's character that stands behind his choosing, purposing, and accomplishing his manifold purposes through Christ's death and resurrection. Telling the story of Christ's work from this vantage point is not merely interesting or helpful. It is certainly not random and obscure. Rather, it stands at the heart of Paul's and ultimately the Bible's understanding of the work of Christ and the fulfillment of God's purposes.

But if it is so central, why do we hear so little about it in the history of the church? The truth is that while this has not been a major theme in the history of the doctrine of the atonement, it has nevertheless played a significant and very interesting role.

---

9. See Ellen T. Charry, *By the Renewing of Your Minds: The Pastoral Function of Christian Doctrine* (New York: Oxford University Press, 1997), 134.

CHAPTER 2

Atonement as a Work of Wisdom: Snapshots from the History of Doctrine

I renaeus, the second-century theologian and bishop of what is now Lyons, France, was deeply concerned with the unity of the Old and New Testaments that was being undermined and attacked in his day.[1] In his account of the story of atonement, the work of Christ was a matter of the unfathomable wisdom of God: "Having received salvation from Him, we continually give thanks to God who, through his abundant, inscrutable and unfathomable wisdom, saved us and preached the salvation from heaven."[2] As Irenaeus understood it, the wisdom of God in Christ consisted in uniting the story of the Old and New Testaments, such that Christ "furnished us, in

---

1. Denis Minns, *Irenaeus: An Introduction* (New York: T&T Clark, 2010), 25-27.
2. Irenaeus, *On the Apostolic Preaching*, trans. John Behr (Crestwood, NY: St. Vladimir's Seminary Press, 1997), 99.

a brief, comprehensive manner, with salvation; so that what we had lost in Adam—namely, to be according to the image and likeness of God ... we might recover in Christ Jesus."[3] Essentially, Irenaeus is saying that Christ, to whom the New Testament bears witness, restores to us what was lost in the Old Testament. The New Testament simultaneously repeats and fulfills its predecessor, a patterned act Irenaeus called "recapitulation" (as in Eph 1:10). The same God works in both, and the same patterns and realities happen in both, but the decisive difference is that Christ, in his wisdom, is the proper fulfillment of the Old Testament.

There are two key insights here: first, the one who saved is the one who created; and second, the failure of God's creation, of his handiwork, would count against the wisdom of God:

> It was necessary, therefore, that the Lord, coming to the lost sheep, and making recapitulation of so comprehensive a dispensation, and seeking after His own handiwork, should save that very man who had been created after his image and likeness, that is, Adam, filling up the times of His condemnation, which had been incurred through disobedience—[times] "which the Father had placed in His own power" [Acts 1:7]. [This was necessary,] too, inasmuch as the whole economy of salvation regarding man came to pass according to the good pleasure of the Father, in order that God might not be

---

3. Irenaeus, "Against Heresies," in *The Ante-Nicene Fathers*, ed. Alexander Roberts and James Donaldson (Peabody, MA: Hendrickson, 2004), 446.

> conquered, nor his wisdom lessened, [in the es-
> timation of His creatures].[4]

By venturing this enterprise, by bringing this creation into existence, God deliberated, purposed, and acted: he exercised his wisdom. He made humans in his image, representing their Creator. But if this creative project were to fail—if the fields were to lie fallow and the rivers run with blood—the wisdom of God would be at stake, since it was in his wisdom that God created. A failure of creation would suggest a failure of God's wisdom. How, then, could God reestablish his wisdom in a fallen world? By both honoring his original creative intent and bringing his creatures to salvation.

For this, the ever-wise God chose to "furnish us, in a brief, comprehensive manner, with salvation ... that what we lost in Adam ... we might recover in Christ Jesus."[5] This manner of salvation was the work of Jesus, which simultaneously honored God's creative intent and brought his creatures to salvation. It honored God's creative intent by giving the creature its dignity—allowing it to remain a creature and allowing it to have a share in its own salvation. Both were fulfilled in Christ, the God-man. Becoming man, God gave his creatures a second chance, a chance to do things right. In doing so, in standing firm and acting righteously where we had failed, Jesus brought us salvation by allowing us to fulfill our purpose.

This is of great importance to Irenaeus, who writes that God chose wisdom instead of power to accomplish his purposes:

> The Word of God, powerful in all things, and
> not defective with regard to his own justice, did

---

4. Ibid., 455.
5. Ibid., 446.

> righteously turn against that apostasy [brought
> on by sin], and redeem from it His own proper-
> ty, not by violent means ... but by means of per-
> suasion, as became a God of counsel, who does
> not use violent means to obtain what He de-
> sires; so that neither should justice be infringed
> upon, nor the ancient handiwork of God go to
> destruction.[6]

Power alone would crush apostasy, but God did not want his handiwork to be destroyed.[7] Rather, he wanted save it—to bring to perfection his treasured creation, with all the worth and dignity he bestowed upon it in the act of creation. But how to redeem a good, free, and rational but horribly fallen creature? Not by power alone, but by persuasion, counsel, and wisdom. Power alone is sufficient for dealing with inanimate objects, but only persuasion and counsel do justice to the delight God has in the freedom and rationality of his creatures. This is the key that unlocks Irenaeus' project of recapitulation, in which Christ repeats and reverses the history of Adam and Eve, Israel, and fallen humankind. He enters their conditions and circumstances and acts righteously, so that in him the history of humankind might be reversed; at the same time

---

6. Ibid., 527.

7. As Hodgson puts it: "Sophia [Wisdom] defines the kind of Spirit that God's Spirit is—not a possessing, displacing, controlling Spirit, but a persuading, inviting, educing, communicating, teaching Spirit, acting in profound interaction with human spirit, indeed the whole cosmos. God's indwelling Spirit has the quality of wisdom rather than of raw force, of education rather than compulsion" (Hodgson, *God's Wisdom*, 93). J. I. Packer, on the relation of power and wisdom, similarly writes: "Power is as much God's essence as wisdom is. ... Wisdom without power would be pathetic, a broken reed; power without wisdom would be merely frightening; but in God boundless wisdom and endless power are united, and this makes him utterly worth of our fullest trust" (Packer, *Knowing God*, 91).

he acts with power and wisdom, in such a way as to save a creature that is rational and free.

In the fourth century, Gregory of Nyssa revisited this question of divine power and wisdom, asking: "Why, then, if he loved man, did he not wrest him from the opposing power and restore him to his original state by some sovereign divine act of authority?"[8] What Irenaeus calls a "brief, comprehensive" work, Gregory here calls a "tedious, circuitous route," noting the stages of the development, life, and death of Christ.[9] While the work of Christ may be brief and comprehensive in comparison to the whole history of sin and corruption stretching back to the fall of Adam and Eve, Gregory is right to point out that it is nonetheless tedious and circuitous in comparison to simple divine fiat, in which God exercises his power and simply makes salvation happen by speaking it into existence — just as he spoke creation into existence in Genesis 1.

His answer highlights the role of divine simplicity, demanding that we think of God not merely in terms of power: "It is universally agreed that we should believe the Divine to be not only powerful, but also just and good and wise and everything that suggests excellence. It follows, therefore, in the plan of God we are considering, that there should not be a tendency for one of his attributes to be present in what happened, while another was absent."[10] Elaborating on the role of divine wisdom, he writes:

> Wisdom, then, certainly needs to be allied with goodness. How is this alliance of wisdom with goodness evident in what happened [in the

---

8. Gregory of Nyssa, "An Address on Religious Instruction," 291.
9. Ibid.
10. Ibid., 296.

> incarnation]? A good purpose, to be sure, can-
> not be detected in the abstract. How then, can
> it be evident except in the actual facts that oc-
> curred? These facts proceed in a logical chain
> and sequence, and exhibit the wisdom and skill
> of God's plan.[11]

God didn't simply save us by his power, because the power of
God does not stand alone; it is fully integrated with the whole
divine character and life, such that it is a good, gracious, just,
and wise power. It is a unique kind of power, the true source
of all power. And because it is the power of his wisdom, it is a
logical, sequential, skilled, and planned kind of power.

How does this help Gregory explain the apparently circuitous method of our salvation? Here, like Irenaeus and Paul
before him, he appeals to the appropriateness of this course
of action by an appeal to the broader, cosmic scope of God's
work—the role of Satan in this drama:

> Now it is the character of justice to render each
> his due. It belongs to wisdom, on the other hand,
> neither to pervert justice nor to divorce its de-
> cisions from the noble end of the love of man.
> Both must be skillfully combined. By justice
> due recompense is given; by goodness the end
> of the love of man is not excluded. ... For it is
> the mark of justice to render to everyone the re-
> sults of what he originally planted, just as the
> earth yields fruits according to the types of seed
> sown. It is the mark of wisdom, however, by the

---

11. Ibid., 297.

> way in which it returns like for like, not to ex-
> clude a higher aim.[12]

Wisdom, in other words, is that aspect of the character of God by means of which he not only exercises his power, not only manifests his justice and stretches forth his goodness, but does these while taking into account his higher aim. It is thus what we might call an orchestrating or strategic attribute. It oversees the weaving together and incorporation of all that God is in a course of action, so that the whole range of God's purposes is brought to completion. Why this circuitous route? Because only such a path could enact the full range of God's character while bringing about the full range of God's purposes. Power alone, justice alone, love alone—none of these, divorced from the others, would in fact be God's action. None of these would be good; none of these would be our salvation. The work of Christ must be a work of wisdom, because only as a work of wisdom does it bring together the whole character of God and the fulfillment of the whole range of God's purposes. To appreciate this insight, we must skip ahead 900 years from Gregory to Thomas Aquinas, one of the greatest synthesizers in the history of the church.

In Thomas, the relation between fittingness and wisdom come to their height in a clear, compelling, and comprehensive story of the atonement. Like Irenaeus and Gregory, Thomas rejects the idea that divine power and will could act alone, because then "the order of divine justice would not have been observed." Accordingly, "Divine wisdom judged it fitting that God should become man, so that thus one and the same person would be able both to restore man and to

---

12. Ibid., 303.

offer satisfaction."[13] Thomas thus employs divine wisdom in the same way as Irenaeus and Gregory: it regulates or brings together the whole character of God (in this case will, power, and justice) in his actions.

What is new is the extent to which Thomas uses this notion of fittingness in his theology; he organizes his thought around the fittingness of the work of Christ—the way that it brings together a whole range of goods relevant to our salvation. Thomas writes:

> Among means to an end that one is the more suitable whereby the various concurring means employed are themselves helpful to such end. But in this that man was delivered by Christ's Passion, many other things besides deliverance from sin concurred for man's salvation. In the first place, man knows thereby how much God loves him, and is thereby stirred to love him in return, and herein lies the perfection of human salvation. ... Secondly, because thereby He set us an example of obedience, humility, constancy, justice, and the other virtues displayed in the Passion, which are requisite for man's salvation. ... Thirdly, because Christ by His Passion not only delivered man from sin, but also merited justifying grace for him and the glory of bliss. ... Fourthly, because by this man is all the more bound to refrain from sin. ... Fifthly, because it redounded to man's greater dignity, that as man was overcome and deceived by the devil, so also

---

13. Thomas Aquinas, *Light of Faith: The Compendium of Theology*, 229.

> it should be a man that should overthrow the
> devil; and as man deserved death, so a man by
> dying should vanquish death. ... It was accord-
> ingly more fitting that we should be delivered
> by Christ's Passion than simply by God's good
> will.[14]

In the subsequent passage, Thomas adds seven reasons
why it was fitting that Christ die on a cross. These include: it is
an example of virtue; it symbolizes the unification of Jew and
Gentile; and it ties in to the Old Testament in a multitude of
ways (something like Irenaeus' recapitulation is in mind here).

The gist of Thomas' move has to do with an analysis of actions and the relationship between a means (how something
is accomplished) and an end (the goal sought to accomplish).
Growing vegetables and raising livestock are means, or ways
of accomplishing, the end or goal of providing food for you
and your family. However, there are a variety of means you
can use to accomplish this end—doing the work yourself, paying someone else to do it for you, or, even less directly, buying
the food from a store. Any number of means can serve the end
of feeding ourselves.

Actions, however, are rarely simple, and a single action can
accomplish any number of ends or goals. Growing sunflowers,
for instance, can (1) provide nourishment for you, (2) provide
nourishment for the cardinals and other birds you enjoy feeding during the winter, (3) make your backyard more beautiful
during the summer, perhaps even (4) provide you with tax

---

14. Thomas Aquinas, *Summa Theologiæ*, trans. Fathers of the English Dominican
Province (Westminster: Christian Classics, 1981), III.46.3.

benefits, should you grow enough of them that it is part of your business, all the while (5) providing food for your family.

Furthermore, actions can be complex. Each action has a range of subactions that serve as a means, accomplishing a variety of ends. Building your own workshop, for example, is a complex action, involving a variety of stages, tools, and skills (carpentry, architecture, finance, etc.). Thomas here explores the crucifixion as an action with a whole host of different aspects, which brings about a whole host of ends or goals. This matters greatly here because the way that the cross serves as a means of bringing together this host of ends is what Thomas calls its "fittingness," and fittingness is precisely what wisdom seeks to discern. Wisdom seeks to determine how a single action can bring to fulfillment a whole range of purposes, thus setting it apart as the best course of action.

In short, Thomas brings together the recapitulation of Irenaeus and the role of wisdom that both Irenaeus and Gregory develop, binding these together by means of a developed account of fittingness. The result is that he can offer one of the most comprehensive accounts of the wisdom of Christ's atoning work up to that point in the history of the church.[15] The work of Christ is not merely just, powerful, or good—it is wise. And it is wise in that by means of this apparently circuitous path, we find a brief and comprehensive solution to God's broken and damaged creation: a single action by means of which God reconciled to himself his whole creation; an action that honored the creature, honored the full reality of the problem of sin and evil, and did so above all by honoring

---

15. For a more detailed account of this subject and how it relates to Anselm's theology, see Adam Johnson, "A Fuller Account: The Role of 'Fittingness' in Thomas Aquinas' Development of the Doctrine of the Atonement," *International Journal of Systematic Theology* 12 no. 3 (2010): 302–18.

the character and purposes of the ever-wise, but equally good, loving, patient, and just God.

Jonathan Edwards is our last stop on this brief historical survey of atonement as wisdom. His series of six sermons entitled "The Wisdom of God Displayed in the Way of Salvation" is noteworthy for several reasons.[16] First, Edwards uses wisdom not only as a part of, but as the organizing feature of his account—an unprecedented move to my knowledge. Second, Edwards' sermons are the most wide-ranging I have seen in terms of the scope of the work of wisdom, bringing together everything we have seen thus far (and then some). Finally, it is delightful to find the preached word so rich and full of insight; reading this collection of sermons is a worthwhile effort in its own right to appreciate the preaching ministry of the church.

Edwards takes as his text Ephesians 3:10 (KJV): "to the intent that now unto the powers and principalities in heavenly places, might be known by the church the manifold wisdom of God." Unlike Irenaeus, Gregory, and Thomas, who brought in wisdom to hold together prior commitments, wisdom for Edwards is the starting point, the premise funding his whole thought project:

> It is called manifold wisdom; because of the manifold glorious ends that are attained by it. The excellent designs, hereby accomplished, are very manifold. The wisdom of God in this is of vast extent. The contrivance is so manifold, that one may spend an eternity in discovering more of the excellent ends and designs

---

16. To be clear, this is not the only way Edwards explores the work of Christ. See S. Mark Hamilton, "Jonathan Edwards, Anselmic Satisfaction and God's Moral Government," *International Journal of Systematic Theology* 17 no. 1 (2015): 46–67.

> accomplished by it; and the multitude and vast
> variety of things that are, by divine contrivance,
> brought to conspire to the bring about those
> ends.[17]

What Edwards adds to our story is a new element having to do with location and emphasis. By placing wisdom at the foundation of his account, the "manifold glorious ends" are highlighted in an unspecified way, opening what is in principle an endless or eternal task to which we can devote an eternity of discovery. Whereas previous theologians used wisdom to synthesize other commitments (reconciling power, goodness, and justice, for instance), here God's wisdom is unleashed, allowed to do its own work prior to any other commitments, enabling the energy and resources proper to wisdom itself to shape and form our understanding of the atonement rather than simply facilitating and contributing to a task set by another agenda. The new element that emerges is the unboundedness, the infinity, the reluctance to specify or limit the number of manifold ends attained by God's manifold wisdom in the cross. What did the ever-wise God achieve in and through the death and resurrection of Christ? The answers are as rich, varied, and endless as the character of God himself, and we could (and will) spend an eternity exploring and delighting in them.

Edwards' sermons are fascinating and merit their own sustained commentary; I will draw on him heavily in the constructive portion of this book. For the time being, it is worth noting that Edwards uses divine wisdom in at least two ways

---

17. Jonathan Edwards, "The Wisdom of God Displayed in the Way of Salvation," in *The Works of Jonathan Edwards*, ed. Henry Rogers, Sereno Edwards Dwight, and Edward Hickman (Peabody, MA: Hendrickson, 1998), 141.

to expand our understanding of the scope of the atonement. First, rather than using it to bring together a set of attributes that otherwise might conflict (as we saw in Gregory), Edwards uses wisdom as the launching point for exploring how each of the attributes plays a role in Christ's atonement.[18] The task essentially is the same, but the direction is altogether different. Rather than a hedging in and unifying move, Edwards uses wisdom in a project-creating move that is inherently expansive and boundless.

Second, as we will see in chapter 6, Edwards employs the wisdom of God to draw out more clearly than before the role of the doctrine of God within the doctrine of the atonement and the extent of creation impacted by Christ's saving work. A good deal of what Edwards writes is to be found in the theologians that we considered earlier, but he gathers and energizes this material by the unprecedented role and centrality he gives to wisdom. This allows Edwards to craft a traditional and orthodox position while simultaneously developing a radically creative and new account of the work of Christ.

---

18. Though I demur from this view, there is some reason to claim that wisdom is in some sense the master attribute within the divine life. Jonathan Edwards, for instance, thinks somewhat along these lines, according to Kyle Strobel, *Jonathan Edwards's Theology: A Reinterpretation* (New York: T&T Clark, 2013). Moreover, "ancient philosophers from Socrates to the Roman Stoics and Epicureans agree that wisdom is the master virtue, necessary for the other virtues as well as happiness" (Rachana Kamtekar, "Ancient Virtue Ethics: An Overview with an Emphasis on Practical Wisdom," in *The Cambridge Companion to Virtue Ethics*, ed. Daniel C. Russell [New York: Cambridge University Press, 2013], 30).

CHAPTER 3

Wisdom, Faith Seeking Understanding, and Theories of the Atonement

The stage has largely been set. The story of atonement as wisdom is not only plausible but warranted both by Scripture and the history of reflection upon it by the theologians and pastors of the church. Before moving on to a definition of wisdom in chapter 4 and sustained development of my own constructive theory of the atonement rooted in divine wisdom and its implications in chapter 5, here I will attend to one more dimension that has lain beneath the biblical and historical work done so far. While the theologians we learned from in chapter 2 helped us see the ways that wisdom actively helps expand our understanding of the manifold work of God in Christ, wisdom also plays another, more subtle role. As it turns out, she isn't always crying out in the streets (Prov 1:20)—sometimes she whispers in the alleys. Specifically, wisdom plays an essential role in developing a doctrine of the atonement in the first place—in trying to understand and reflect on the reasons motivating God to act as he has.

Without wisdom there may be a reconciliation of God, humankind, and creation, but there can be no doctrine of the atonement, no understanding of this work on the part of the church. As Barth says, "because [God's] Word is His wisdom, because the power of His Word is, therefore, the power of His wisdom ... [God's word] is not a closing but an opening of our eyes. It is not suspension of the real knowledge of God, but the basis of it."[1] Because God's work and word are the work of his wisdom, they allow for, invite, and lead to our knowledge and understanding. Theirs is a work of revelation, laden with meaning and purpose that we can and should appreciate, consider, and dwell upon. There is such a thing as doctrine—the attempt to think God's thoughts after him, to make sense of his actions in history. This is so because God's actions have sense (they are logical and full of meaning), and he does in fact think thoughts that he wishes us to think after him, that we might come to know and understand him.[2] There is such a thing as doctrine, as theology, because God is wise and his actions are the work of that wisdom.

Suppose that during Mary, Joseph, and Jesus' escape to Egypt, Roman soldiers rushed by on horseback. Jesus was knocked to the ground and trampled to death, only to rise from the dead three days later and ascend into heaven. Jesus would have been fully God and fully man, and could have borne our sins. Surely his work would have been just as effective—so what would have been different? While the major elements are in place for Jesus' atoning work, our witnessing of

---

1. Barth, *Church Dogmatics* II/1, 423.
2. Ibid., 424–32.

this event, and therefore our understanding, is left out of the picture. We do not get to witness the key events, and are left without the opportunity to reflect and dwell upon what has happened and its implications. God is concerned not merely to save us, not merely to do something for us that we could not do ourselves, but to bring us into a relationship. He wants to allow us to witness, and on that basis to know, understand, and therefore worship him as the one who has done these things for us and for our salvation.

Why then do we engage in this reflection? Why does God want and equip us to do this? Why ask questions about what God has done? Surely we need only know and believe that Jesus Christ, the risen Lord, forgives our sins, right? As the Carpenter in Chaucer's "Miller's Tale" says:

> God has some secrets that we shouldn't know.
> How blessed are the simple, aye, indeed,
> That only know enough to say their creed![3]

In short, is there any need for, or benefit from, discussing God's will and purposes, the reasons behind this event? Surely the abundance of theology books (this one included) testifies not only to the richness of God but also to the division, error, and perhaps hopelessness of the theological task?

It should not be surprising that I believe there are a host of reasons to affirm our desire not merely to trust but also to understand. Here I will mine one of the deepest and richest veins in this treasure-laden shaft, exploring the role of the wisdom of God—broadly in the very enterprise of doing

---

3. Geoffrey Chaucer, *The Canterbury Tales*, trans. Nevill Coghill (New York: Penguin, 2003), 95.

theology, and more specifically in the theological study of the work of Christ.

The answer to the question of why we engage in theological reflection lies deeper than the benefits we receive, deeper than any longings we might have—far deeper, in fact, than anything to do with humankind whatsoever. We begin with the joy of God: the joy he has in his own wisdom and his joy in sharing his wisdom with his creatures, both that they might appreciate it and partake of it. The root of this joy is the fact that God in himself is both wise and the source of wisdom, as Pseudo-Dionysius affirms: "Now, if you will, let us give praise to the good and eternal Life for being wise, for being the principle of wisdom, the subsistence of all wisdom, for transcending all wisdom and all understanding."[4] With him "are wisdom and might; he has counsel and understanding" (Job 12:13), and in this wisdom God made all his works (Psa 104:24): he "made the earth by his power ... established the world by his wisdom, and by his understanding stretched out the heavens" (Jer 10:12). But just as God does not cling to his honor and status (Phil 2:5–11), neither is he stingy with his wisdom but seeks to share it, "for the LORD gives wisdom; from his mouth come knowledge and understanding" (Prov 2:6); in doing this he blesses "the one who finds wisdom, and the one who gets

---

4. Pseudo-Dionysius, *The Complete Works*, trans. Colm Luibheid (New York: Paulist Press, 1987), 105. Kant writes: "*Wisdom* ... dwells in God alone; and the only thing which could perhaps be called human wisdom is acting in a way which is not visibly contrary to the idea of that [divine] wisdom." (Immanuel Kant, *Religion within the Boundaries of Mere Reason*, trans. Allen W. Wood and George Di Giovanni [New York: Cambridge University Press, 1998], 202). Along the same lines, Packer writes: "Wisdom is, in fact, the practical side of moral goodness. As such, it is found in its fullness only in God. He alone is naturally and entirely and invariably wise" (Packer, *Knowing God*, 90).

understanding" (Prov 3:13).[5] Wisdom is not a gift that is foreign to or distant from himself, something that is of assistance to us but of no intrinsic relation to God, the source of our well being; rather, in giving us his wisdom, God gives us himself.

The central locus of this self-revealing, self-sharing, and creature-blessing work of God is Jesus Christ. He is the one on whom the foretold Spirit of the Lord rests in wisdom, counsel, and might (Isa 11:2), the one greater than Solomon (Matt 12:42), the one calling Jew and Gentile together, who stands before us as the "power of God and the wisdom of God" (1 Cor 1:24), with "wisdom and insight" that is not merely effective but is lavished upon us (Eph 1:8). But this lavishing, this blessing that God bestows on us is no mere sideshow within his plan for creation: His intent was "that through the church the manifold wisdom of God might now be made known to the rulers and authorities in the heavenly places" (Eph 3:10). In other words, it is the cosmic purpose of God to shower us with his wisdom, and therefore this is at the heart of the longing of Paul for the people of God.

This is why the prayers and doxologies of Paul are saturated with wisdom language: "I keep asking that the God of our Lord Jesus Christ, the glorious Father, may give you the Spirit of wisdom and revelation, so that you may know him better" (Eph 1:17 NIV); "We continually ask God to fill you with the knowledge of his will through all the wisdom and understanding that the Spirit gives" (Col 1:9 NIV); and: "Oh, the depth of the riches of the wisdom and knowledge of God! How unsearchable are his judgments and how inscrutable his ways!" (Rom 11:33). Once more, Paul writes: "My goal is that

---

5. On the link between wisdom and Phil 2, see Daniel J. Treier, *Proverbs & Ecclesiastes*, Brazos Theological Commentary (Grand Rapids: Brazos, 2011), 50–51.

they may be encouraged in heart and united in love, so that they may have the full riches of complete understanding, in order that they may know the mystery of God, namely, Christ, in whom are hidden all the treasures of wisdom and knowledge" (Col 2:2–3 NIV).[6]

This paints a compelling picture in which the ever-wise source of all wisdom, who exercised his wisdom in the creation of all things, longs to share with us his wisdom—his very self. He has done so in the Law and the Prophets, but the culmination of this self-revealing and self-sharing work of wisdom is the life and work of Jesus the Messiah. In him God showers us with wisdom, inviting us into his life of wisdom that we might grow in wisdom, understanding, and knowledge. But this is no abstract or merely philosophical or cultural wisdom; it is a wisdom gained only by knowing and understanding Jesus Christ, in whom are hidden all the treasures of wisdom and knowledge. The whole story of wisdom thus revolves around Jesus Christ; he is the center, the means, the source—simply put, he is Wisdom.

How does this affect our project? Theories of the atonement are nothing less than the attempt of the church to understand the wisdom of God in Christ and to appreciate and participate in this work. This is an achievable task, because even though God is "unsearchable [in] his judgments" and his ways are

---

6. Barth writes of this verse: "As a knowledge of God as well as man, as a looking back to God's election, creation and covenant, and a looking forward to His coming eternal kingdom, it converges upon [Him] from every side... It is therefore true that Christ is the mystery of God, that all the treasures of wisdom and knowledge are hidden in Him and not elsewhere (Col. 2:3). Why? Because He who has been appointed by God the beginning of all knowledge is also the One who decides its total compass. It is, therefore, only at the risk of immediate and total blindness that we separate ourselves from it." Karl Barth, *Church Dogmatics* IV/1: *The Doctrine of Reconciliation*, ed. G. W. Bromiley and T. F. Torrance (Edinburgh: T&T Clark, 1988), 81.

"inscrutable" (Rom 11:33), he has showered himself upon us in Christ and his Spirit. To develop a theory of the atonement—to seek to understand the work of Christ by delighting in the enacted wisdom of God—is to share in the blessings God has for us, to fulfill Paul's longing that we might share in the wisdom of God.[7] Put differently, the wisdom of God enacted in Christ does not rest contented in being effective or in bringing us blessings. It does not resent our questions or our attempts to understand, because we share in the blessings of wisdom precisely by becoming wise; this happens as Wisdom draws us into himself, allowing us to probe the mystery and delight in the wisdom, understanding, and knowledge of God. And this is precisely what we seek to do as we, in faith and prayer, contemplate the death and resurrection of Christ.

Why do we develop the doctrine of the atonement? Why do we elaborate theories of Christ's reconciling work? Because Christ died so that we might enter his wisdom by seeking to understand its enactment in him. Christ died and rose again so that we might develop theories of the atonement as an act of faith seeking wisdom.

And while the primary truth must be that Christ died and rose again so that we might enter his wisdom, we must also acknowledge the darker side of his work: God became man so that in his life and death he might bear the full reality and consequences of our folly. While we may be tempted to think of a fool as merely a jester or someone who is stupid or silly, this falls far short of what Christ bore for us and for our

---

7. My hope is that in part this addresses Charry's critique that "throughout the Western church, enjoying God was gradually marginalized to become the province of sporadic mystics. ... One result of this loss was that it is virtually impossible for Western Christians to see the social and ethical implications of formation through the enjoyment of God" (Charry, *Renewing*, 129).

salvation. Folly that unintentionally destroys precisely that which it seeks, that unleashes harm for the most piteously avoidable and unnecessary reasons, that was simultaneously so needless and disastrous that we can only weep in stunned disbelief and horror—this was our sin. This was how we treated the good gifts of God. Christ came that he might take upon himself our folly and suffer its full and disastrous reality and consequences.

Why did God become man? So that he might take upon himself our folly and its consequences. And what is more— what is far more—so that in turn he might grant us a share in his wisdom through our participation in his resurrection.

CHAPTER 4

Defining Wisdom

S o far we have seen that the doctrine of the atonement is a matter of telling the true story of Jesus' life, death, and resurrection in ever new and faithful ways, and it necessarily involves our careful selection of what we will and will not tell. In the doctrine of the atonement, it is our emphasis on a divine attribute that shapes the primary features of the doctrine and largely determines the unique features of our telling of the story. In order to offer the broadest and most expansive story of the atonement, and partly to move past Gustaf Aulén's massively influential telling of the tale, I have chosen to shape the story from the perspective of divine wisdom. This is just one vital way of telling the story, which we must go on to tell and retell from other vantage points.

As an aside, this telling and retelling of the story is not primarily driven by culture or our perceived needs but by faithfulness to Scripture's own varied telling of the work of Christ. For example, in a pastoral context we should consider the fittingness of the particular way we tell of the work of Christ, but we should not allow context to be determinative.

Pastoral sensitivity merely plays a (vital) role in what is ultimately a matter of faithfulness to the biblical witness. It does
not determine or constrain the telling; it merely provides the
connection by means of which we begin telling of Christ's
work, which we then expand by other tellings called for
by Scripture.

To begin this story of the atonement as divine wisdom,
I will first consider wisdom as an attribute of God. In the
following chapter, I will explore wisdom's role in relation to
Christ's atonement.

WISDOM IN THE LIFE OF GOD

There is no shortage of writings on the nature of human wisdom.[1] But what of *divine* wisdom, the wisdom that is unique
and specific to the triune life of God? This, after all, is the source
of any other reality we might call wisdom. Philosophical and
psychological observations regarding human wisdom are at
best suggestions and pointers to be affirmed or challenged by
God's self-revelation in Scripture.[2] Christian theology does
not project human values and virtues onto God; rather, it
attends to the enacted character of God in the history of his

---

1. Daniel Treier, for example, writes that wisdom is "cleverness or instrumen-
tal skill, about a human moral judgment, about a quest to live in harmony with
the order of creation, or about a prudence incorporating all of the above *after*
beginning with 'the fear of the Lord.'" ("Wisdom," in Kevin J. Vanhoozer et al.,
eds., *Dictionary for Theological Interpretation of the Bible* [Grand Rapids: Baker Academic, 2005], 844). Roberts and Wood write that wisdom is a practical, or "aiming"
virtue: "it posits ends or an end to be achieved through the actions that it guides"
amidst "a variety of situations," implying "an element of improvisation in the
exercise of practical wisdom." (Roberts and Wood, *Intellectual Virtues*, 306). This
entails wisdom as a living responsibly and well within "the interwovenness of
the world and humanity and God." Daniel W. Hardy, "The Grace of God and Earthly Wisdom," in *Where Shall Wisdom Be Found? Wisdom in the Bible, the Church, and
the Contemporary World*, ed. Stephen C. Barton, (Edinburgh: T&T Clark, 1999), 231.
2. Pseudo-Dionysius, *The Complete Works*, 105.

self-revelation, using human language to witness to the character he reveals.

And according to Scripture, God is wise. God is the "only wise God" (Rom 16:27), a God of "manifold wisdom" (Eph 3:10). His creation was a work of his wisdom (Prov 8:23–31; Psa 104:24–26; Jer 10:12; Col 1:15–20). And this wisdom is powerful and active, for throughout Scripture wisdom is paired with both power and understanding (Job 12:13, Psa 33:10–11). God seeks to make his wisdom known to the powers and principalities through its realization in the work of Christ (Eph 3:9–11), and we praise him for the depths of his wisdom, knowledge, judgments, and ways (Rom 11:33). This wisdom confronts and triumphs over the false wisdoms of the world (1 Cor 1:20–24).

To put it most generally, that God is wise means that God lives well—God lives masterfully. As Bruce Waltke puts it, "'Wisdom' (ḥokmâ) means generally, 'masterful understanding,' 'skill,' 'expertise.'"[3] In keeping with Waltke's location of his definition of wisdom within his definition of life itself,[4] it follows that wisdom, understood most broadly, is a matter of having "masterful understanding of life," or being "masterfully skilled at life." And God, who is the source of all wisdom, who is "wisdom's sole possessor,"[5] is the one who is masterfully skilled at life, and as such lives well.

Put more fully, that God is wise means that God lives well by bringing about the full range of his purposes by the most fitting means, taking full account of the whole array of

---

3. Bruce K. Waltke and Charles Yu, *An Old Testament Theology: An Exegetical, Canonical, and Thematic Approach* (Grand Rapids: Zondervan, 2007), 913.

4. Ibid., 908–10.

5. Ibid., 919.

circumstances and factors surrounding him.[6] As Father, Son
and Holy Spirit, God is the living God, the one who in and of
himself lives, moves, responds, and acts—the one in whom is
life (John 1:4): "To its very deepest depths God's Godhead consists in the fact that it is an event—not any event, not events in
general, but the event of His action."[7] Unlike false gods, who
are lifeless, static, and motionless, ours is a living God. His existence is that of event—a living, active, and powerful event or
history.[8] And because God is wise, he lives well: for him to be
the living God and the wise God are one and the same. All the
Proverbs, all the wise sayings that guide us to a life well lived,
have their source and origin in a living God who in himself
lives well, and created that he might share with others a life
well lived (e.g., Prov 1:33; 2:6-8; 3:5-6).

---

6. See Karl Barth, "The Beginning of Wisdom," in *Deliverance to the Captives* (New
York: Harper & Row, 1961), 127; Marcus Aurelius, *Meditations*, trans. Robin Hard
(New York: Oxford, 2011), 67; cf. Kevin J. Vanhoozer, *The Drama of Doctrine: A
Canonical-Linguistic Approach to Christian Theology* (Louisville: Westminster John
Knox, 2005), 308; Waltke and Yu, *An Old Testament Theology*, 913.

7. Barth, *Church Dogmatics* II/1, 263. "This is no metaphor," according to Barth,
but "describes God Himself as the One He is. 'As I live' or 'As the Lord ... liveth' is
not for nothing the significant formula for an oath in the Old Testament. God is
'the living fountain' (Jer. 2:13, 17:13), 'the fountain of life' (Ps. 36:9). The Father has
life in Himself (Jn. 5:26). Christ is 'the author of life' (Ac. 3:15), even 'the life' (Jn.
14:6, Phil. 1:21, Col. 3:4, 1 Jn. 1:2), and 'eternal life' (1 Jn. 5:20), 'alive for evermore'
(Rev. 1:18). The Holy Spirit is life (Jn. 6:63, Rom. 8:10). All this is clearly in contra-
distinction to the gods and idols who 'have no life' (Jer 10:14, Ac. 14:15)." He goes
on to write that "In speaking of the essence of God we are concerned with an act
which utterly surpasses the whole of the actuality that we have come to know as
act, and compared with all that we have to know as act is no act at all, because as
act it can be transcended. This is not the case with the act of God that happens in
revelation" (ibid.; cf. ibid., 257-72, esp. 271-72).

8. It is because he is living and active that he can say: "Fear not, for I am with
you; be not dismayed, for I am your God; I will strengthen you, I will help you, I
will uphold you with my righteous right hand" (Isa 41:10), that his word "shall not
return empty," and he will accomplish that which he purposed (Isa 55:11), that he
is able to work things for the good of those he loves (Rom 8:28), that he is able to
make "the world and everything in it" (Acts 17:24).

For God to live well is also for him to reject chance or ca-
price. His will is "meaningful in itself," since God "knows not
only what He wills, but why and wherefore He wills it," which
is to say that his willing is bound up with "plan and intention."[9]
To say that God lives well is to say that he lives fully; he lives
a fulfilled life in which the full range of his purposes is met.
This is a life of full perfection, in which God is conserved in
his own end, because there is no conflict between end, means,
and fulfillment for God. They are all rooted in, accomplished
by, and fulfilled in himself as Father, Son, and Holy Spirit.[10]
God does not need to seek food, shelter, or pension, because
he has all he needs within himself—his action springs forth
out of the fullness of his perfect life; fulfillment is intrinsic to
the divine act rather than a striving toward it as a distant and
perhaps unachievable goal.

But to speak of ends or purposes is to speak of means—the
methods, tools, or resources by which a purpose is brought
to completion. What means does God employ in his wisdom,
in his living well? Surely nothing outside of himself, no person, angel, or created reality would do, since then God would
rely on something other than himself for his own perfection,
entailing an intolerable dependence of God upon his creation.
But if God does not rely on something other than God, then
on what does he rely? Surely it is the divine life itself.[11] God is

---

9. Barth, *Church Dogmatics* II/1, 423.
10. Thomas Aquinas, *Prologue to Aquinas's Commentary on the Sentences* (http://
dhspriory.org/thomas/Sentences.htm). Thomas writes: "The fourth thing that
pertains to the wisdom of God is *perfection*, whereby a thing is conserved in its
end. Take away the end, and only vanity remains, which wisdom cannot suffer
to abide with her."
11. Friedrich Schleiermacher is helpful here, in his warning that "we must be on
guard lest we ... introduce the contrast of end and means. The reason for caution
lies in [the fact that] ... every human work of art is the more perfect, the more
it conforms to the idea that elements within it should not be distinguishable as

his own means to living out his life in the fullness of his perfection. God lives out the divine life by means of the divine
life. God is not alone, not without resources, not dependent
on others for his fulfillment. As Father, Son, and Holy Spirit,
God is able to be the means by which he is who he is. This
is true in the eternal begetting of the Son by the Father and
the breathing forth of the Spirit, and also in the shared life
in which Father, Son, and Holy Spirit relate to each other,
enacting the divine character in eternity. God, in his wisdom,
uniquely lives well by being the means through which he lives
his divine life, accomplishing his divine purposes.

But to accomplish a purpose, you have to employ certain
means within a context, within certain circumstances. What
are these circumstances within the life of God? Again, nothing
but himself.[12] God's life of wisdom is the Father's eternal begetting of the Son and breathing forth of the Spirit; in it God
lives his life well (the Father) by means of himself (the Son)
and in relation and unity with himself (the Spirit). Whereas
we set goals for ourselves that are not ourselves, with God it is
altogether different. God is God's own goal, which he accomplishes in eternity by means of himself. God lives out his life
by means of himself, before and in relation to himself, because
he fully knows, understands, and rejoices in himself. As the

end and means, but are all reciprocally related as parts to the whole; whereas
the means remain external to it." He continues, "Means are never employed
except where the agent has to have recourse to something not originated by
himself." Friedrich Schleiermacher, *The Christian Faith* (Edinburgh: T&T Clark,
1968), 733-34.

12. In this section I am exploring in my own terms the territory charted by
Augustine in *The Trinity*, book VII. There Augustine makes wisdom a relational
reality within the life of God, akin to the relation between Father and Son, or
speaker and word, so that God is not merely wise as a matter of being; he is wise
as a matter of relationship. The very dynamics of the Trinity are the dynamics
of wisdom, and the basis for our ascribing wisdom to God. What does it mean for
God to be wise? For him to be Father, Son, and Holy Spirit.

triune God, he is able to be himself by means of himself and in relationship to or knowledge of himself. Wisdom, as Barth puts it, is "the inner truth and clarity with which the divine life in its self-fulfillment and its works justifies and confirms itself"—but confirms itself to itself, in self-fulfillment.[13] God's wisdom is God living his life on the basis of his self-knowledge, properly ordering himself and his actions so as to continually bring about his purposes by means of himself, so that there is a continual and limitless well-living on the part of God in and for himself.

And just as God's own triune life is the basic pattern of wisdom, so Father, Son, and Holy Spirit fully enact the divine wisdom. It is not merely the case that God the Trinity is wise or the pattern of wisdom; because the one, undivided essence of God exists in no other way but the eternal processions and relations, each person is described by Scripture as being wise. God is the only wise God (Rom 16:27), Jesus the incarnate Son is the wisdom of God (1 Cor 1:24), and the Spirit is the Spirit of wisdom and understanding (Isa 11:2). Just as the Trinity contains within itself the dynamics of wisdom, so each of the members fully enacts those dynamics. And we know all this about the inner life of God by working backward, from the self-revelation of God enacted in the person and work of Jesus Christ—a move he intends and wills us to make, because he wills to be known by us, and acts within history so as to make himself known. Put differently, God acts within history that he might be feared, and precisely this fear is the beginning of wisdom.[14]

---

13. Barth, *Church Dogmatics* II/1, 426.
14. Along these lines, see Job 28:20–28.

In summary, God's wisdom is God's living well. He lives well by bringing about the full range of his purposes by the most effective and fitting means, given a thorough understanding of the whole spectrum of relevant circumstances. This wisdom, though powerfully enacted in the work of Christ, is at the same time—and as its basis—a reality within the inner life of God, a description of the relation between Father, Son, and Holy Spirit. As we describe God in his wisdom, we do not attribute something to him that is foreign to his inner life as God. Rather, in speaking of the wisdom of God we are delving into the very heart of God, the internal relational dynamics of the Trinity in which God is who he is by means of himself, in knowledge of or relation to himself. God, in himself, is wise, is the source of all that we call wisdom.

Wisdom in Relation to Creation

God lives well both in himself and in relation to his creation. And in creation as in eternity, the triune God is a purposeful God. He creates and sustains with the particular aim of bringing about the intensions he wove into the fabric of his creation. His is an ordered and purposeful life, and he saturates his creation with order, meaning, purpose, and intent. For God to be the wise God is for him to bring his creatures to their fulfillment in him such that the purpose, meaning, and order he gave them is made "very good." For God to be wise is for him to know how to bring his creative project to completion. Throughout Scripture we find a continuous unfolding of God's purposes, whether with regard to the divine name (John 12:28), glory (Phil 2:11), or a whole host of other purposes, all of which God brings to completion in the work of Jesus, the Messiah of Israel.

But God does not merely bring about his purposes; he does so by means of the proper or fitting means, through the most fitting and appropriate methods, tools, and resources. Like a craftsman plying his trade, God knows the right tool for the job and the consequences of the wrong choice. Throughout Scripture, we see God using angels, animals, stars, men, women, and children to bring about his purposes—but most of all, we see him using himself. "I myself will do this," and as a result, "you will know that I am the LORD" resounds throughout the book of Ezekiel (for example, Ezek 17:21-22; 34:11; 37:13), and the work of God's "mighty arm" likewise reverberates throughout the Psalms (Psa 77:15; 89:13; 98:1). God is a God who brings about his purposes by means of his creation, by means of the leaders, judges, prophets, and kings that he establishes—but above all and most decisively by means of himself. The miracles of the exodus, the parting of the Red Sea, the feeding of Israel in the wilderness, the conquest of Jericho—the Old Testament is laden with stories in which God stands as the sole and exclusive source of the salvation of his people. He does this so that he might simultaneously rescue them from peril, make himself known to them, and bring them to the promised land. Our God is a God who makes himself the means of bringing about his purposes—a God of preparation, strategy, and fitting action.

And God's purposes are brought about by the most fitting means within a context or set of circumstances. In this case, the context is the whole of creation, and in particular the powers and principalities mentioned in Ephesians and Colossians (which form the broadest scope of circumstances in Scripture). God, who is the Creator, the source of all that is, knows everything he has created and sustained. Therefore he is fully and completely able not only to know all things but also to act wisely, given his perfect and complete grasp not only of that which he wants to bring about and the way he wants to do so but also of the host of factors relating to that decision.[15] An expert mountaineer might know herself, her equipment, the mountain, and the weather, but with God there are no unforeseen consequences, no surprise side effects—he is the source, sustainer, and goal of all creation. The ever-wise God acts on the basis of his full and complete knowledge,[16] and thereby acts knowing that his step is sure, his foot steady, and the action he seeks to accomplish will reach its conclusion. He knows that there is no constraint or disruption, no sphere outside his knowledge, understanding, and lordship that could impinge on the success of his plans. For him there is no lack of evidence calling for cutting babies in half (1 Kgs 3:25); there are no riddles to outsmart him.

In sum, our God is a wise God who lives out his purposes by means of and in relation to himself. Therefore he also brings his purposes in creation to fulfillment by means of himself, and lives well in relation to himself and the whole scope of his treasured creation. And because God is a God of wisdom, because his whole being and life is a being and life of wisdom, it follows that his history with us exudes that same wisdom. On the basis of this conviction, we must now ask how the death and resurrection of Jesus, his atoning work, is a work of wisdom. More precisely, how is Christ's atonement a work by, of, and for Wisdom?

---

15. Pseudo-Dionysius, *The Complete Works*, 107.

16. The connection between God's wisdom and knowledge is an intimate one throughout Scripture. The essential difference is that wisdom pertains to activity, while knowledge pertains to epistemology. Ultimately, of course, they are as inseparable as God's patience and his goodness.

CHAPTER 5

Atonement:
A Work by, of,
and for Wisdom

With this material in place, we have everything we need to craft a theory of the atonement rooted in the divine wisdom—a *sophiological* theory of the atonement, we might say.[1] This is needed because, while theologians and pastors throughout the history of the church have employed wisdom to think about the work of Christ, no one has pulled this material together in quite this way. In this chapter, I will make the case that the death and resurrection of Jesus Christ is a work by, of, and for wisdom, in which Wisdom incarnate bears in himself the full reality and consequences of creation's folly in his death, so as to reestablish it in wisdom through his resurrection.

---

1. I borrow the term *sophiological* from Charry, *Renewing*, 130.

A Work by Wisdom

First and foremost, atonement is a work performed by Wisdom. God himself, the ever-wise God, did not hold the world at arm's length, but drew it near to himself. In the incarnation of the Son, God brought the fullness of the divine life among us, brought the fullness of divine wisdom among us. Everything I have said about wisdom so far, every characteristic of wisdom within the triune life of God, every aspect of wisdom as God has enacted it throughout the Old Testament and the history of his covenantal interactions with his people—all of this came, became flesh, and dwelt among us (John 1:1-14).[2] God had shared his wisdom with his people through his judges, prophets, and kings; through poetry, wisdom sayings, and stories; through crafting his creation wisely. But these means, these ways of accessing wisdom, were insufficient. They were unworthy of the intimacy with which God sought to share himself. Or rather, they were preparatory for God's great purpose of sharing his wisdom, sharing himself, with us. The work of Christ, therefore, is not merely a wise work, a work that bears in it the characteristics of wisdom. Rather, this is the work of Wisdom himself—a claim with at least three profound implications.

First, this is the great and decisive revelation of divine wisdom, the source of all wisdom. Here there is no mediation, no loss of content: Wisdom itself is active in Christ, not merely crying in the streets (Prov 1:20) but conversing with the people, healing the sick, and bearing the cross.[3] It is by

---

2. The linguistic ties between this passage and divine wisdom are made all the stronger by the role of the *Logos*—a concept bearing strong affinity to wisdom.

3. Schleiermacher has a provocative interweaving of wisdom and revelation, in which "the most perfect man" is he "whose plans for works or actions formed a complete whole of self-communicative presentation. Similarly, the divine

the standard of incarnate Wisdom in the person and work of Jesus the Messiah that we judge every form of human wisdom; it is with this plumb line that we determine the relative straightness or crookedness of the philosophies and heritages of the lands (1 Cor 1:18–31).

Second, this is the light that exposes all partial wisdom,[4] false wisdom, scheming, cleverness, and cunning,[5] whether they are corrupted by the purposes they seek, the means they employ, or their disastrous limitation of the circumstances they consider. While human wisdom navigates toward happiness through the pressures and circumstances of life, divine wisdom enacted within history contains the further and definitive dimension of revelation: "Through the wisdom of God the hidden things of God are made manifest and the works of creatures are produced, and not only produced, but restored and perfected."[6]

Third, because this is a revelation of wisdom and exposure of folly (or false wisdom), it is at the same time an invitation, a pathway into a life well lived. To treat this revelation of life well lived as a mere subject of knowledge would be a horrible irony—a tragic reduction of wisdom to mere knowledge. This

---

wisdom is nothing but the Supreme Being viewed as engaged in this absolute … self-presentation and impartation" (Schleiermacher, *The Christian Faith*, 733). Along these lines, John of the Cross writes (though not in immediate connection with wisdom) that "true lovers are only content when they employ all they are in themselves, all they are worth, have, and receive, in the beloved; and the greater all this is, the more satisfaction they received in giving it" (John of the Cross, "The Living Flame of Love," in *The Collected Works of St. John of the Cross* [Washington, DC: Institute of Carmelite Studies, 1979], 673).

4. Plato tells us of the fault of the good craftsmen: "Each of them, because of his success at his craft, thought himself very wise in other most important pursuits, and this error of theirs overshadowed the wisdom they had." Plato, "Apology," in *Complete Works* (Indianapolis: Hackett, 1997), 22d–23.

5. Barth, "The Beginning of Wisdom," 127.

6. Thomas Aquinas, *Selected Writings*, trans. Ralph McInerny (New York: Penguin, 1998), 51.

will not do, because Christ did not come merely that we might know about the Father but that we might know him. This is a lively and relational knowledge, a life well lived with the Father, a life of wisdom, wherein the fear of the Lord and the living of life are bound together as a seamless garment.[7]

But God became man for a far wider range of purposes than enacting and revealing wisdom in our midst, exposing false wisdoms, and drawing us into a life well lived in him. Wisdom, in living well, is effective; it accomplishes its purpose with fitting and appropriate means, taking into account the full range of circumstances. And this is precisely what we see not merely in the life, but also in the death and resurrection of Christ: God's great restorative work of wisdom.

A Work of Wisdom: The Goal

What was Christ's purpose in his death and resurrection? Can we limit it to just one? He came to seek the lost, heal the wounded, feed the hungry, fulfill the Law and the Prophets, triumph over Satan, complete the role of the temple, cleanse the defiled, satisfy the honor of God while bringing honor to the shamed, adopt us, bring to completion the work of Adam, restore creation to its Edenic state, pay our ransom, descend into hell, be the propitiation and expiation for our sin, fulfill the sacrificial system once and for all, reconcile Jew and Gentile, share with us his Holy Spirit, bring to an end the groaning of creation, be our bride price, bear in himself the covenantal curses and promises, suffer the exile of Israel—and is this list

---

7. Charry uses Augustine to establish that "in the ancient world, knowing something implied tasting it—indeed, participating in it. ... Augustine pressed Christians not just to celebrate what God has done for them but also taste and enjoy God. And since the 'essence' of God is justice, wisdom, love and goodness, participation in these qualities is eternal life with God" (Charry, *Renewing*, 133).

complete? Far from it! How then can we speak adequately of Christ's purpose in his death and resurrection? A moment's thought leaves us speechless.

Yet speak we must, since the purposes of the Lord will stand (Prov 19:21). So what shall we say? It is best to begin with as broad a statement as possible, like the simple profession of love and faithfulness in the marriage vows that serves as a prelude to a more complete, lifelong unpacking of this love. We affirm broadly, then, that through his death and resurrection Jesus Christ sought to bring the full range of his creative purposes to fulfillment, reconciling all things to himself (Col 1:20). Nothing is left out. The new creation is as expansive as the first. The Creator, in the act of creating, saturated his creation with purpose and meaning. The fall disrupted not only our own standing before God but also the whole order and harmony of creation. The problem was cosmic in scope, calling for an equally cosmic solution. God's purpose in the atonement, in other words, is bound up with his purpose in creation—they are one and the same, except that the latter has to do with a restoration in the face of sin and evil (*recreatio ex corruptio*) while the former was a more straightforward creation out of nothing (*creatio ex nihilo*).

Such a train of thought puts us firmly in the mindset of Athanasius, one of the greatest early expositors of Christ's saving work:

> As we give an account of this [salvation], it is first necessary to speak about the creation of the universe and its maker, God, so that one may thus worthily reflect that its recreation was accomplished by the Word who created it in the beginning. For it will appear not at all

> contradictory if the Father works its salvation
> in the same one by whom he created it.[8]

Drawing on the logic of 1 Corinthians 1:15–23, Athanasius offers an unparalleled elaboration on the fact that the same one who created all things was the one who effected the reconciliation of all things: Jesus Christ. All the joy, intentionality, and anticipation were not merely God's but were woven into the very fabric of creation, such that what it means to be a creature is to be what God made us to be and to be called to fulfill what God intended for us. To be a creature is to be shaped and determined not only by what we are but also by what our Creator meant us to be. And it is this same God—the ever-faithful God who does not abandon his purposes but brings them to completion in his wisdom—who became man that his purposes for creation might be fulfilled. Why did God become man? To restore his creation.[9]

Such a restoration entails the triumph of God over all the powers opposing him; the perfection of the creature, including the overcoming of all guilt, shame, dishonor, and the many other guises of sin, corruption, and death; the restoration of order within the heavenly realms, including but not limited to the angels; and the rejoicing and glorifying of the earth now groaning and longing for the liberation and manifestation of God's children in their glory. Such is the scope of God's purposes in the work of Jesus Christ. This emphasis on the massive scope and range of purposes provides the context for appreciating the wisdom of Christ's work. Purpose is an

---

8. Athanasius, *On the Incarnation*, trans. John Behr (Yonkers, NY: St. Vladimir's Seminary Press, 2011), 53.
9. On the faithfulness of God, see this resounding theme throughout N. T. Wright, *Paul and the Faithfulness of God* (Minneapolis: Fortress, 2013).

essential feature of wisdom as it seeks to accomplish goals amidst the relevant conditions and circumstances by the most efficient or fitting means possible.

A Work of Wisdom: The Efficient Means

As a work of wisdom, the atonement does not rest content with purpose alone. Wisdom's concern is to bring purpose to completion, to satisfy the original plan or intent of the maker. And while a fool seeks shortcuts, which often make for long delays,[10] the wise seek a path in keeping with the nature of things—a means of bringing about the goal, taking great care to account for the full range of factors involved. While the fool may hasten to build a house, the wise take account of a whole range of factors, including the foundation on which the house is built (Matt 7:24-27). What seems like needless delay as one surveys the land and considers the changes of the seasons, proximity to the road, water table, neighbors, or other factors, ultimately pays rich dividends both in losses avoided and efficiency gained. One modern example of this truth comes from Bruce Waltke, who tells of the Westminster Theological Seminary library and its unfortunate placement atop one of the world's largest known concentrations of radon gas![11]

Given that Jesus is Wisdom incarnate, how are his death and resurrection an effective means to accomplish this work? The first thing to note is that the wisdom required for efficiency increases dramatically with every additional goal. A wedding, for instance, could be a relatively simple affair: a bride, a groom, some vows, a blessing, and some witnesses. But as

---

10. And according to Frodo Baggins in Tolkien's *Fellowship of the Ring*, "Inns make longer ones."

11. Waltke and Yu, *An Old Testament Theology*, 917-18.

has happened with many a wedding, the goals start piling on: gift registry, save the date and formal invitations, pictures, a video, friends and family flying in from out of town who need accommodations and entertainment, estranged family members who want to come but refuse to be near each other, pressing demands from work, the church that cannot accommodate Grandma's wheelchair... The list goes on and on, turning a beautiful and potentially simple event into a whirling icon of the complex intermeshing of two lives in marriage. Only wisdom, in the form of a wedding planner, can guide and coalesce this into the beautiful ceremony and event it should be.

The range of purposes entailed in Christ's atonement far transcends that of the most elaborate wedding party. After all, this is the grand wedding party, the fulfillment of creation and the covenants as the groom comes to claim his wayward bride.[12] And his chosen means of bringing about his purposes—of effecting them—is himself. Nothing less than the full resources of the divine life are adequate. Nothing less than the whole being and life of God as Father, Son, and Holy Spirit in the fullness of the divine perfections serves as the source and means to bring about his purposes.

But at the same time, nothing less than the full redemption of the creature will do. God's plan was not merely for God to triumph, for God to do what he wanted to do. Power alone would suffice for this—no elaborate schemes are necessary. A word alone (though perhaps a "deplorable word"[13]) would suffice to end this creation and make a new one its place. But this would not satisfy or glorify God. For his purposes to

---

12. See Ezekiel 16 and the book of Hosea in their relation to Ephesians 5, and how all of these culminate in Revelation 21.

13. See C. S. Lewis, *The Magician's Nephew* (New York: Macmillan, 1964), ch. 5.

be made good, for him to be well pleased, it was necessary to him that the creature, God's covenant partner, participate in this work—this is what God sought in the first place. Nothing less than God could bring about this work. And nothing less than humankind, God's covenant partner, playing our role, would satisfy God. And this is the dilemma of wisdom: only the full resources of God could bring this about, and only the full participation of the creature could please God.

Wisdom's solution was to become incarnate, to become a man and to make literal the walking and speaking of wisdom in the streets (Prov 1:20). The full resources of the being and life of God, and the full participation of the creature, were bound together so as to make good the plan of God. There was no impossible task for humankind, no abandoning of the plan on God's part—the two, bound together, made an otherwise impossible act possible through this union.[14]

But this is not all, because a full humanity and full divinity do not make a full Christology. While Jesus is fully man, he is at the same time fully creature; as such he plays the role not merely of man but of representative creature before God such that every creature, physical and nonphysical, finds itself (and its fate) in God and God alone. According to some medieval theologians, a Messiah could not represent angels to atone for their sin. The reason is that they did not have "kinds"; each constituted its own species, such that a Messiah could not be born "of their kind."[15] Nevertheless, as the crown of creation and the one who has authority over angel and demon alike, Christ is also bound up with the nonphysical creation, and they too find their fate bound up in him. Fully man, made of

---

14. A parallel to this point is the union of the Suffering Servant and the Messiah.
15. See Thomas Aquinas, *Summa Theologiæ* I.50.4.

earth, Christ binds up and represents the whole of creation: earth, animal, humankind, and angel, the fate of the whole is bound up in him.

And through his substitutionary and representative death, Christ effects the demise of all of fallen creation—a fact testified by the darkened sky itself in the Gospel narratives. In God's wisdom, nothing less than the destruction of creation would honor the reality and consequences of our folly, while nothing less than the full perfection of creation would honor the even greater reality and consequences of God's purposes and covenants. How then to honor both? Through the representative and substitutionary work of Christ, who takes our place, the place of fallen creation, in his death (substitution) and, simultaneously, the one in whom we ourselves and creation as a whole die (representation). God, in his wisdom, made himself the means of fulfilling his purposes, binding to himself the reality and fate of the creature, so that in his experience of death on the cross the death of all might be effected, and that in his resurrection all might be perfected.

A Work of Wisdom: Circumstances

Because God is wise and attends to both his purposes and the best means of achieving them, he likewise attends to the circumstances of this work—this too is an essential component of wisdom. One of the ways Scripture develops this theme is through the idea that God became man "at the right time" (Rom 5:6; Gal 4:4). Precisely what this means is debatable, but the point remains that according to Paul there was an appropriateness or fittingness to the time God chose for this work. Partly this may have to do with the fulfillment of prophecy, another theme bound up intimately with the wisdom of God.

Beyond that, however, the work of Christ takes into account a whole range of relevant circumstances in addition to those considered above when discussing God's purposes. For instance, Jesus lived a full life. Rather than briefly taking up human flesh and being sacrificed for our sins at the hands of the Romans at a young age, Jesus grew, matured, and entered a public ministry for several years. In the process he lived the life into which he invites us, creating the pattern in which we are to walk through his Spirit. Moreover, he lived an Israelite life, keeping the law, fulfilling the prophecies, and keeping God's covenant with his people.

Why does this matter? After all, he could have paid the penalty for our sins in any number of ways, in any number of contexts or time periods. Why as an Israelite? Because God, in his wisdom, is attentive to all the circumstances and factors that in any way touch on this event. He is attentive to his people Israel and will not abandon his covenants with them. He is attentive to our limitations, needs, and the knowledge he wishes us to have of him, and so lived a full life with us that we might see and hear and touch him (1 John 1:1). He is attentive to time, taking it into account in his planning and orchestrating the work of Jesus Christ. He is attentive to the individual, social, and political realities of both sin and salvation, and so Jesus lived a public life, interacting with widows and governors, confronting demons and being watched by angels. All of creation observed its Lord publicly, for this was a public work that was meant to be observed, understood, and appreciated.

Wisdom's Parody: The Sin of Folly

To complete our reflection on atonement as a work of wisdom, we surely must add a parallel line of thought, a vital aspect of the circumstances surrounding the work of God's wisdom: our sin, or more particularly, our folly. The character of God manifest within the work of Christ casts a light that exposes sin, revealing it as a disastrous parody of the divine character. Insofar as God is a wise God and his works are works of wisdom, the cross exposes our sin as folly. A longing for (illicit) wisdom was at the heart of our fall (Gen 3:6) and collapse into death (Prov 2:18-19), and Israel's sin is characterized as a foolish affront to the Creator (Deut 32:6). It was an act of folly on Saul's part that cost him his kingdom (1 Sam 13:13-14), and a similar act by David cost Israel dearly (1 Chr 21:8). Folly is not hidden from God (Psa 69:5), but leads to suffering (Psa 107:17), ruin (Prov 10:8, 10), punishment (Prov 16:22 NIV) and death (Prov 5:23). Folly, as Proverbs sees it, is a wholesale rejection of God, which God in turn utterly spurns and rejects (Prov 1:22-32). Personified, Folly is a mistress seducing us deep into the realm of the dead (Prov 9:13-18). Jesus builds on this Old Testament theme, weaving foolishness into his parables (Matt 25:2), lumping it in with adultery, greed, malice, deceit, lewdness, envy, slander, and arrogance (Mark 7:22 NIV). Paul weaves it into the fabric of his account of the depravity of humankind in Romans (1:21-22), pits folly against a participation in the things of the Spirit (1 Cor 2:14; Gal 3:3), and puts it at the head of a list describing our sinful condition prior to our salvation through the washing of that same Spirit (Titus 3:3).

Folly, in sum, is completely rejecting God and turning away from him as the source of all wisdom. It is our attempt to actively determine our own sources and standards of wisdom, or passively and slothfully embrace the pleasures and pains of

living apart from God.[16] We see it in children who stubborn-
ly pursue paths they find attractive, failing to see the harm
and consequences attending them. We see it in a husband
walking away from his family into a relationship everyone
recognizes as a temporary and unsatisfying fling, resulting
in far more pain and suffering than pleasure and fulfillment.
Such choices are more than disastrous, unleashing ruin, disaster, and death; they are culpable. They are a rejection of
God and his wisdom, on the one hand, and the way of wisdom
he created us to walk in on the other. They are a stubborn and
willful decision to ignore the wisdom and insight of God and
friends, running into disaster, attending only to an unstable
and poorly crafted mirage of promise. Folly, alongside guilt,
shame, disobedience, and a host of other descriptors for sin,
is an accurate and enlightening summary of our fallen, self-
inflicted condition before God. To be a sinner—to depart from
and reject the character and way of God—is to be a fool.

In this awareness of sin as foolishness we have an insight
of profound personal and pastoral application. Just as we are
plagued by guilt, shame, and unfaithfulness (as are those
around us), so we play the fool, and our lives and those of
others are drastically affected by folly. Folly leaves the aching
feeling of preventable loss, such as the pain and confusion resulting from a spouse who gambled away hard-earned savings,

---

16. We have in view here the folly contracted, as Thomas says, "by plunging [our]
sense into earthly things, whereby [our] sense is rendered incapable of perceiving Divine things, according to 1 Cor. ii. 14." Even though no one wishes such a
condition direction, "he wishes those things of which folly is a consequence, viz.
to withdraw his sense from spiritual things and to plunge it into earthly things"
(ibid., II-II.46.2). Kant explains this "plunging of sense into earthly things" as a
matter of using "means to their ends which are directly opposed to these ends"
(Kant, *Religion within the Boundaries of Mere Reason*, 202; cf. Wood's section
on "Lookalikes, Counterfeits, and Opposing Vices of Prudence" in Wood, "Prudence," 47–49).

or the grief over a friend's lifelong running after things that cannot satisfy, leaving a trail of wreckage behind. We are consumed with folly and plagued by its consequences—the culpable, avoidable litany of disastrous decisions pulling down ruinous consequences upon ourselves and everyone around us, including generations to come.

Ironically, the final vengeance folly wreaks on us appears to be a form of wisdom. As the Greek playwright Sophocles tells us at the end of *Antigone*:

> Our happiness depends
> on wisdom all the way.
> The gods must have their due.
> Great words by men of pride
> bring greater blows upon them.
> So wisdom comes to the old.[17]

But this "wisdom" gained by the end of this tragic play, this wisdom that comes to the old, is a hideous wisdom. It is an understanding of the way things could have been, or should have and would have been, were it not for folly. This wisdom is no longer able to effect good, because those whom it could help have already been destroyed by folly. It serves only to bend and crush the old in the weight of its hindsight. There is no joy in this wisdom—no life to be lived well. There is only the ability to look downward and backward, tormenting the fool in his old age.

And why do we suffer so greatly at the hands of fools, including ourselves? For a bit of honey and a drop of oil:

---

17. Sophocles, *Sophocles I: Antigone, Oedipus the King, Oedipus at Colonus*, trans. David Grene (Chicago: University of Chicago Press, 1991), lines 1347–1352.

My son, give attention to my wisdom,
Incline your ear to my understanding,
That you may observe discretion,
And your lips may reserve knowledge.
For the lips of an adulteress drip honey,
And smoother than oil is her speech;
But in the end she is bitter as wormwood,
Sharp as a two-edged sword.
Her feet go down to death,
Her steps lay hold of Sheol.
She does not ponder the path of life;
Her ways are unstable, she does not know it
(Prov 5:1–6 NASB).

It is important to point out that the honey is genuine and the oil is real. The promises are fulfilled, since though the devil is the father of lies, he also keeps his word. The trick lies not in his falsehood but in the deal as a whole, the big picture. Where the fool sees ease and wisdom, the wise cast an eye about, perceiving where Lady Folly's feet lead. Where the fool sees a free meal, the wise sense a trap. Where the fool sees a surefire path to a quick fortune, the wise sniff out danger. Where the fool snatches at expediency, the wise take the sure path, attended as it may by weeds and thorns, giving every indication of being the path not taken (Matt 7:13–14).

The power, the ruin, lies not in what is sought or grasped. It lies in the pitiable exchange: saving five minutes at the cost of a speeding ticket or a life, having a moment of sexual gratification in exchange for the family and marriage one has been building up for decades, seizing the opportunity to win a battle at the expense of ultimately losing the war. What makes folly foolish is not that which is grasped—it is the other end of the deal, the tragic fine print that always catches up with us in the end:

> Suddenly he follows her
> As an ox goes to the slaughter,
> Or as one in fetters to the discipline of a fool,
> Until an arrow pierces through his liver;
> As a bird hastens to the snare,
> So he does not know that it will cost him his life
> (Prov 7:22–23 NASB; cf. Prov 9:17–18).

But Jesus, who bore our sin, bore our folly.[18] Those who mocked him on the cross saw something real. Christ suffered derision from the "wise" of this world because he played the fool or became the fool, bearing our folly and its full consequences just as he bore our guilt. He brought upon himself our disaster, ruin, punishment, and death. He felt the consequences of Eve's rash grasp for wisdom, and suffered the fate of the fool described throughout Proverbs, in our place treading into the depths of Lady Folly's house. This is not to say, of course, that he was foolish. While he was perceived as a fool, he is in fact Wisdom and acted wisely—but only when viewed from the perspective of God's purposes and plans for creation as a whole.

This is the blessed "foolishness" and "weakness" of God (1 Cor 1:25), that God in Christ took upon himself not only our weakness but our folly, and chose this in his wisdom as the means by which to triumph over our false wisdom and power. Just as with the prophecy of Caiaphas (John 11:50) and Christ's crown and inscription on the cross ("This is the King of the

---

18. Barth comes close to making this claim but, in an atypical move, turns to judicial language at the crucial point (Barth, *Church Dogmatics* II/1, 434).

Jews," Luke 23:38), so too with the "foolishness" of Christ—the Gentiles, ironically, were right! Christ did become our foolishness that he might suffer its consequences in our place. It was not in the wisdom and grace of God to allow us to reap the full harvest of our folly.[19] This vintage he reserved for himself, drinking this bitter cup to the dregs (Matt 26:39).

A Work for Wisdom

To end here with Christ's crucifixion would be folly great enough to earn a sequel to Erasmus' classic work *In Praise of Folly*—such a faith is useless, as Paul says (1 Cor 15:14). The death of Jesus is no more the goal of God's work than is engagement for the betrothed, running sprints for the football player, or the operating room for the injured. The purposes of God do not and cannot end in death, the final enemy to be overcome (1 Cor 15:26). Death, deprived of its sting, itself becomes a means, a blessing, a transition to life. As George Herbert writes in his poem "Death":

> Death, thou wast once an uncouth hideous thing,
>   Nothing but bones,
>   The sad effect of sadder groans:
> Thy mouth was open, but thou couldst not sing.
>
> For we considered thee as at some six
>   Or ten years hence,
>   After the loss of life and sense,
> Flesh being turned to dust, and bones to sticks.

---

19. Charry tells us of an epigram in which "the self is formed by creation, deformed by sin, and reformed by Christ" (Charry, *Renewing*, 131). In the present context, I would adapt this to: "the self is formed by Wisdom, deformed by folly, and reformed by Wisdom incarnate."

We looked on this side of thee, shooting short;
    Where we did find
The shells of fledge souls left behind,
Dry dust, which sheds no tears, but may extort.

But since our Saviour's death did put some blood
    Into thy face;
Thou art grown fair and full of grace,
Much in request, much sought for, as a good.

For we do now behold thee gay and glad,
    As at doomsday;
When souls shall wear their new array,
And all thy bones with beauty shall be clad.[20]

The primary power and efficiency of Christ's atonement do not lie in his death, for death is but an "uncouth hideous thing." Rather, the power and efficiency of Christ's atonement lie in his resurrection. On this side of the resurrection, death has a new countenance, a new hue. Color has been put in his face, and he has become a friend, full of favor and grace.

As Paul tells us in 1 Corinthians 15, if Christ were still dead we would be in our sins (1 Cor 15:17). But through his resurrection he has brought about the firstfruits of his work, which is the resurrection of all and the putting of all things under his feet, so that God may be all in all (1 Cor 15:20–28). If there is no resurrection, then Christ has not been raised. And if Christ has not been raised, our preaching and faith are useless and futile; we are false witnesses, and most pitiable (1 Cor 15:13–19). While the language of folly does not appear in this passage, it

---

20. George Herbert, "Death," in *The Works of George Herbert* (London: George Routledge & Co., 1853), 198–99.

is "in the water." Folly is useless, and the striving of the fool is futile; they lack the effectiveness of wisdom. The fool is pitiable and bears false witness. (Bear in mind the correlation of fools and false witnesses throughout Proverbs.) In short, if Christ has not been raised, we are fools who are still in our sins. The wisdom of God is not the way of the cross! It is the way of the resurrection through the cross.

We again find ourselves in the domain of wisdom in Paul's letter to the Philippians:

> But whatever were gains to me I now consider loss for the sake of Christ. What is more, I consider everything a loss because of the surpassing worth of knowing Christ Jesus my Lord, for whose sake I have lost all things. ... I want to know Christ—yes, to know the power of his resurrection and participation in his sufferings, becoming like him in his death, and so, somehow, attaining to the resurrection from the dead (Phil 3:7-8, 10-11 NIV).

This is wisdom language, because it is by wisdom that we reprioritize our understanding of gains (Prov 11:28; 22:1). And wisdom and power go hand in hand; they have their meaning only in and through each other as mutually complementary descriptions of the activity of the triune God (Job 12:13; Dan 2:20; Matt 13:54; 1 Cor 1:24).[21] The wisdom of God that is on display in the crucifixion is also found in the power of the resurrection; this above all is the end and goal of God's work in Christ—his work by, of, and for wisdom.

---

21. Packer, *Knowing God*, 91.

The resurrection is the vindication of God's purposes, the work of his wisdom effectively bringing creation to fulfillment by means of his own activity in human flesh. The resurrection is the firstfruit of the new creation, and Christ is the firstborn of the dead (Col 1:18). This is the beginning, the remaking of creation—and this time things are the way that they were meant to be. The resurrection of Jesus is the triumph of God, the work in which all things are, are being, and will be made right. The resurrection is the goal and fulfillment of Christ's atoning work, the act of recreation by the Creator, the finale to the great undoing and destruction of fallen creation in the crucifixion of Jesus.[22]

This is precisely one of the places where our theology of the atonement is most dreadfully incomplete. Anselm's famous work on the atonement, *Cur Deus Homo* (*Why God Became Man*), explores Christ's work at length but never mentions his resurrection. We preach the cross as though the death of Christ itself were a good thing, but all this is meaningful precisely because of the resurrection! Formal education is relevant for the ways in which it prepares us for life moving forward. A tool is good because of the work it helps us do. An engagement is beautiful for the union it anticipates. But without the life, the work, the relationship, all these things are as useless as a creation that lies fallen into sin, evil, and corruption. God's delight, first and foremost, is in the sharing of himself with his restored creation in the power of the resurrection. This is the good news; this is the good gift he has to share with us.

---

22. As Barth writes: "For them, Jesus Christ the Crucified, in whom they have their being from God, as God's children, has made by God Himself by His resurrection, not only justification, sanctification and redemption, but also and above all wisdom ([1 Cor 1] v. 30), in order that in them may be fulfilled the words of Jer. 9:23ff.: 'He that glorieth, let him glory in the Lord'" (*Church Dogmatics* II/1, 436).

But as we await the return of Christ and the full manifestation of that which was inaugurated and accomplished in the resurrection, we live between the times. We take up our cross daily, but do so in the power of the resurrection. This is why Paul speaks of knowing the power of the resurrection and then the participation in Christ's sufferings (Phil 3:10); the latter occurs only in the power of the former for the church. There is still a way of suffering to be trodden in this present life, still a role for following in the path of the suffering Messiah. The cross is not merely the means of overcoming sin, to be discarded the first chance we get. The cross, while overcoming sin, is simultaneously the pattern of life, both in the present age and the one to come—the pattern of Wisdom incarnate.[23]

What does this look like? We embrace suffering, to be sure, but not as though suffering were in itself a good or effective thing. Suffering is as effective as the cross; that is to say, apart from the power of the resurrection it is folly: utterly vain and powerless. God became man, suffered, died, and rose again, that in Christ his people might be established in his wisdom, treading the way of the cross together in the power of the resurrection. We enter and share the pain and suffering of others, not for the sake of suffering, but for the sake of the freedom and joy and life that the risen Christ brings. We voluntarily embrace conditions of affliction, not because such a posture is good, Christian, or meritorious, but because we, as the church of God, are equipped to inhabit such circumstances in a way that powerfully and effectively witnesses to the gospel

---

23. See Jeremy R. Treat, *The Crucified King: Atonement and Kingdom in Biblical and Systematic Theology* (Grand Rapids: Zondervan, 2014).

of the risen Christ.[24] We are free to respond to manipulation, bitterness, and sarcasm with a joy and kindness so free from anger that it just might disorient the person we love into a state of openness and vulnerability—preludes to repentance, growth, and charity.

The Christian life is energized and shaped by the same fundamental reality that created the world and then re-created it in the person and work of Jesus Christ: the Wisdom of God.[25] Transformed in Christ, the Wisdom of God, the church is equipped for a life of wisdom, understanding, and discernment in which it purposes to act in wise and fitting ways, glorifying the ever-wise God. There should be no shirk-ing of this calling, no lapse into folly, since God has called the bride of Christ to a life of wisdom—including but far transcending the calling of Proverbs 31. We must be a people who, in the power of the Spirit of God, cherish, cultivate, and demonstrate wisdom. Nothing less is a reasonable and fitting response of worship (Rom 12:1) to the ever-wise God who, in and through his wisdom, brought us out of our folly for lives of wisdom in him.

But there is no guarantee that such wisdom will be per-ceived as such. Some may be crowned as true philosophers

---

24. This is important to note in light of one of the chief criticisms of feminist theology with regard to the atonement. Inasmuch as Christians embrace suffer-ing, punishment, pain, and death per se as good things, as though this were fol-lowing in the footsteps of Christ, the feminist critique is rightly made. But to do this is not to follow the way of Christ. Christ's suffering and death were effective because they were bound up with the wisdom and power of God. To follow in the way of Christ is to enter suffering in the power of the resurrection as the people of God in the power of the Spirit to fulfill the will of God. This is a far cry from horrific situations were victims remain in situations of abuse because "suffering" alone is the will of God.

25. "The soul cannot see herself in the beauty of God unless she is transformed into the wisdom of God, in which she sees herself in possession of earthly and heavenly things" (John of the Cross, "Canticle," 612).

or lovers of wisdom, but far more likely we will be scoffed at by those who see nothing but folly in our actions of love and service. As Sophocles tells us, foolishness is often "in a fool's eye."[26] The label "philosopher" can be accompanied, as it was in the case of Socrates, by a drink of hemlock.[27] And we may think this way about ourselves even as we obey our wise Lord, shocked at the apparent folly of our actions, trusting and hoping that the wisdom of God will emerge victorious. The path may be wise, but accolades will be few. The crowds, after all, saw little to appreciate in our Lord whose actions we seek to faithfully and creatively emulate in the present day.

This is just as true of the life of the mind as it is of enacted wisdom. As in the days of Solomon, we are to make our ear attentive to wisdom and incline our hearts to understanding, calling out for insight and raising our voices for understanding, seeking it like silver and searching for it as for hidden treasures (Prov 2:1–4). The one difference is that for us the fear of the Lord is bound up with person and work of Christ: the fear of the risen Lord is the beginning of wisdom. We should be eager to question, hungry to explore the reality of things, and thirsty for wisdom, understanding, and insight into all the fields of study opened to us by God's creative work. This ranges from theological study to physics, healthcare management, and the history of Portuguese colonialism. We should explore these in awareness of and under the lordship of Christ, with an eye to how they shape and inform the Christian life. We dare not ignore wisdom and the activity to which it is bound, since we ignore them only by rejecting the nature and calling bestowed on us by our Lord.

---

26. Sophocles, *Antigone*, line 470.
27. See Plato's *Apology* and *Phaedo*.

Summary: Atonement as a Work by, of, and for Wisdom

The atoning work of Christ is the definitive revelation of wisdom. According to Scripture, wisdom is not merely a human virtue, an abstract concept or good to strive for. Rather, wisdom is a characteristic of the life of the triune God—and this God became man in the person of the Son, fully enacting the divine wisdom for us in the life of Christ.

Because Christ is Wisdom incarnate, his work is a work of wisdom—a work that bears all the characteristics of wisdom as it is effectively enacted for us. In Christ's work, Wisdom incarnate makes itself the means of fulfilling its purposes, bringing its creation to fulfillment by bearing in itself the full reality and consequences of our folly through the crucifixion and death of Jesus Christ—an event that, ironically, the world could only understand as folly.

Because this work was by and of wisdom, it was also for wisdom. In the power of the resurrection, Jesus brings the church into the full inheritance of the wisdom God intended to share with his creatures in the first place. Accordingly, the church ought to be a wise people whose individual lives and actions are richly and deeply characterized by wisdom.

It remains for us to consider the benefits or implications of such an approach to the atonement of Jesus Christ. These will prove to be richly significant, as one might expect of such a wise work. In the remainder of the book, I will explore the benefits of this view for appreciating the breadth of Christ's saving work, lay out the consequences for how we approach debates about the doctrine of the atonement, and point toward the way that this project challenges us to redefine—or at least expand—our typical definitions of wisdom.

CHAPTER 6

Wisdom and the Breadth of Atonement: In Dialogue with Jonathan Edwards

A pproaching the atonement from the standpoint of divine wisdom takes us deep into the doctrine of creation—to its very beginning, in fact (Prov 8:22–31). From there, the doctrine of atonement can be developed with continual reference to creation, for wisdom is just as concerned with achievements as it is with original purposes. The unfolding of God's wise purposes within creation provides the essential elements of the doctrine of atonement. To develop this material, I will take up the thread dropped at the end of chapter 2, drawing heavily on the thought of Jonathan Edwards as found in his collection of sermons "The Wisdom of God Displayed in the Way of Salvation."[1]

---

1. All references to Jonathan Edwards in this chapter come from Edwards, "The Wisdom of God Displayed in the Way of Salvation." I offer a much fuller treatment of this topic in chapter 6 of *Atonement: A Guide for the Perplexed.*

Because of wisdom's connection with the very roots of all things and the manner in which God brings them to fulfillment, the doctrine of the atonement unfolds in a uniquely expansive way in this soil. While other approaches to the atonement have their strengths, we are uniquely helped to appreciate the breadth and range of this doctrine when we see it through divine wisdom. Again, an image helps to explain how approaches to the atonement relate to one another. To fight a battle, it is helpful to see the enemy's lines from a higher vantage point. Today we use satellites, while in years past, such as during the Civil War, armies experimented with hot air balloons. While such a strategic view of the battle is useful, it is not necessarily the best or most important. For example, a thorough understanding of the psyche and history of the opposing general might provide equally valuable information. Both are part of an overall grasp of the circumstances we would want to have in a battle.

Atonement is the epic synthetic project of bringing all things together in Christ. It is God's work of re-creation, and therefore just as expansive as the first creation.[2] Because re-creation is as expansive as creation, the atonement is first and foremost about the one accomplishing the atonement, just as creation is first and foremost about the Creator: Father, Son, and Holy Spirit.[3] Just as in creation, God is on full display in the atonement. Just as God spoke (Gen 1:1–2:3), and the Spirit hovered over the waters (Gen 1:2), and creation was

---

2. In fact, Edwards suggests that in a sense, re-creation is *more* expansive than God's original act of creation, because while creation was out of nothing, re-creation—or atonement—was out of conflict and opposition from fallen creation, and the great opposition of Satan (144).

3. On the relation between the doctrine of creation and the doctrine of the Creator, see Barth's delightful treatment in *Dogmatics in Outline*, 50–58.

made through the Word (John 1:3), so Christ's work is done by the will of God (John 3:16) through the person of the incarnate Son (John 1:14) in the power of the Holy Spirit (John 1:32–33, Luke 4:1). And in the resurrection, Jesus returns to the right hand of the Father (Mark 16:19; Acts 2:33), and receives the promised blessing of the Spirit (Acts 2:33; Mark 1:9–11) that he might share it with his body and bride, the church (Rev 22:17).

The work of re-creation is a work of conflict, in which God willingly faces the power of folly and death—and it is in conflict that wisdom shines most brightly. Atonement, God's act of wisdom-in-conflict, is not merely a second act of creation but the ever-wise God's further commitment to love his fallen and rebellious creation by restoring it to wisdom. It is a further involvement of God in the lives and existence of the creatures he had called into being. And for that reason, it is a further revelation and manifestation of himself as the wise God: Father, Son, and Holy Spirit, each fully active in this work. As Edwards puts it:

> Each person of the Trinity is exceedingly glorified in this work. ... The Father appoints and provides the Redeemer, and accepts the price of redemption. The son is the Redeemer and the price. He redeems by offering up himself. The Holy Ghost immediately communicates to us the thing purchased; yea, and he is the good purchased (145).

Here the veil is pulled back and what was present in creation is fully made known: the full enactment and glorification of each person of the Trinity in God's creative and saving economy.

This is just as true of God's character as it is of his person, for the whole point of creation was for God to manifest and share his life with the creature. Just as God created the heavens to show forth his glory (Psa 19:1), righteousness (Psa 50:6), power (Psa 68:34), and faithfulness (Psa 89:5), so this same God parted the heavens and came down (Psa 18:9 and Phil 2:5–11), bringing his glory, righteousness, power, and faithfulness with him. And while, as Edwards says, "all his works praise him, and his glory shines brightly from them all," nevertheless:

> … as some stars differ from others in glory, so the glory of God shines brighter in some of his works than in others. And amongst all these, the work of redemption is like the sun in his strength. The glory of the author is abundantly the most resplendent in this work. Each attribute of God is glorified in the work of redemption (144).

From this general reflection, Edwards proceeds to elaborate briefly the ways in which the power, justice, holiness, truth, mercy, and love of God are glorified in this work (144–45). These are just a few of the attributes of God found throughout Scripture, and this insight is equally true of all of them. We would do well to expand Edwards' insights as we seek to glorify the God who shared his glory with us in the work of Christ.

But Christ's work of wisdom extends far beyond the self-enactment and self-revelation of God. The whole of creation, the full realm under the providence of God, is fully in play as well, for the work of Christ is the grand synthesis, the bringing together of all that God is and all that he presides over in his providence so that all things might be reconciled in him. Nothing is left out—no corner of creation untouched. This is the re-creative work of the Creator, Wisdom bringing to fulfillment wisdom's creative work by means of itself, Wisdom incarnate.

To this end, Edwards even climbs to the heavens to consider the work of Christ for angels: "It is for men that the work of redemption is wrought out; and yet the benefit of the things done in this work is not confined to them, though all that is properly called *redemption*, or included in it, is confined to men. The angels cannot partake of this, having never fallen; yet they have great indirect benefit by it" (147; cf. 141). Given that the angels never fell, how might they benefit from Christ's work? First, they benefit from contemplating the glory of God revealed in this work, since such contemplation is their chief occupation. Edwards writes, "Perhaps all God's attributes are more gloriously manifested in this work, than in any other that ever the angels saw"—especially with such attributes as mercy, which have no occasion for manifestation in heaven (147). Second, they benefit in that Jesus by this work becomes their head as the God-man (147, citing Col 2:10; Eph 1:20-22). Third, "the elect of mankind are gathered into their society" such that the "heavenly society" becomes all the greater (148). Fourth, it gives angels all the more reason to prize their own happiness by seeing what it cost to secure ours (148). While the angels were not saved from their sin, they were nevertheless brought to a greater perfection in and through the wise work of Christ.

Edwards also dives into the depths to consider the ramifications of the work of Christ for the fallen angels. For those creatures utterly and finally opposed to God and his will, the work of Christ brought about those vestiges of peace and reconciliation that were possible. He utterly frustrated their wicked designs and used their condition as a means for further glorifying God: "By this contrivance for our redemption, God's greatest dishonor is made an *occasion* of his greatest glory" (148). At the same time, Satan's greatest contrivance proved to be the means of his own undoing, the "instrument of frustrating his own designs" (152).

We learn two things about God's wisdom from this. First, the wisdom of God uses even those who are utterly and irreversibly opposed to his will to triumph over them. He brings about his purposes, frustrates their own designs, and brings what semblances of peace and reconciliation are available to those implacably entrenched against the kingdom of God: confinement, the enactment of law and justice in the form of punishment, and the limitation of their ability to do further evil and harm to others. Second, the wisdom of God is in direct contrast to the "contriving" of Satan (which echoes the craftiness of the serpent in Genesis 3), reminding us of the subtle perversions of God's wisdom that so powerfully shape the lives around us.

Christ's work of wisdom also affects the part of creation between angels and demons: humankind. This work of Christ, precisely because it is a work of wisdom, purchases for us all that we need. Through his shed blood, God satisfies his justice and appeases his wrath so that we might have peace with him. This peace is not merely an escape from hell but a "satisfying happiness," providing for "the capacity and craving of our souls" (145). Salvation, in order to be what God intended it to be, had to be holistic. "Man has a natural craving and thirst after happiness; and will thirst and crave, till his capacity is filled. And his capacity is of vast extent; and nothing but an infinite good can fill and satisfy his desires" (145). Along these lines, Christ's work provides for our relational, volitional, and affective needs—for this work is fundamentally positive, even if it includes the destruction of all the negative and sinful aspects of our lives and being. In sum: "In this way of salvation, provision is made for our having *every sort of good* that man naturally craves" (146).

Angels, demons, and humans are not the whole of God's creation. What of animals and plants, and the earth as a whole? Paul tells us that the whole of creation is groaning in labor (Rom 8:22), so though Edwards does not touch on these matters in these sermons, we can fill out portions of the picture he left incompletely painted. Just as the unfallen angels are brought to greater perfection, and just as our bodies are perfected through the resurrection of Christ in which we participate, so creation itself is affected by Christ's death. It is not saved from its sin, for like the angels, creation itself has no sin. But like the angels, creation needs to be rescued from the consequences of sin, from its groaning (Rom 8). The resurrection and glorification of Christ's body provides the framework for understanding the recreation of all things, that they might be made well and whole. The fate of God's animals and the earth generally is similar to that of Christ's pre-resurrection body, now awaiting the recreation and glorification that will come with the resurrection of the dead.[4]

---

4. I am here following the logic of Rom 8:18–25, which binds together the fate and groaning of creation with our own glorification, which in turn is bound up with the glorification of Jesus Christ, and his return.

Edwards teaches us that the work of Christ meets our deepest longings and provides for the fullness of our needs as humans, but it does far more than that. The death and resurrection of Jesus Christ are the solution to a problem that extends far beyond anything to do with humankind. Angels and demons, the earth and the creatures that walk upon it—all of these are bound up with the fate of the maker of heaven and earth, who in the person of the Son become a creature that he might take upon himself the groaning of creation, restoring it to its purpose in himself.

Of course, this centers on the fate of humankind, since in his purposes God first elected to become Jesus Christ, a man (Eph 1:4). But as a man he is the Lord of his creation, and the fate of the whole rests in him. If we contemplate Christ's work and its implications for the whole of creation, we will gain a full and proper context for appreciating the many ways Christ's death and resurrection affect us according to our kinds, our races, our communities, our families, our souls, our bodies—the whole of humankind.

CHAPTER 7

Wisdom, Atonement, and Polemics: Reconciling the Atonement

T hus far wisdom has guided us on an exploration of Christ's atoning work, helping us to appreciate a wealth of biblical and theological material that has often been ignored or underutilized in standard accounts of the doctrine. We have seen a powerful theme of wisdom flowing throughout the canonical story, including Paul's provocative move of intertwining it with the death and resurrection of Jesus. We have likewise witnessed major theologians throughout the history of the church using divine wisdom as a core aspect of their development of the atonement. Building on these trends, I have advanced what might be called a "wisdom theory of the atonement," in which Christ's atonement is a work by, of, and for wisdom: Jesus, Wisdom incarnate, took upon himself our folly and its disastrous consequences so that, in and through our resurrection in him, we might be established in lives of wisdom.

We have explored a number of benefits to this approach. First, wisdom explains and thus further motivates the very attempt to understand the work of Christ—apart from the wisdom of Christ's work, there would be nothing to understand, no meaning after which we could search. There would be gracious benefits, perhaps, but no understanding and its corresponding love, thanksgiving, and worship. Second, seeing atonement from the standpoint of wisdom propels us toward a more full integration of the creative and re-creative project of God. It demands and facilitates our interweaving the Old and New Testaments, on the one hand, and motivates our exploration of the benefits of Jesus' death and resurrection for the whole of God's creation, on the other. As we have seen, the fact that both creation and re-creation were accomplished by the same agent—by the ever-wise God, by Wisdom himself—has profound consequences for the scope of God's re-creative activity. Third, this approach urgently calls and equips the church for a life of wisdom, because we were saved by and for nothing less than participation in the wisdom of God.

In this chapter, I will develop a further application of this book's thesis: Understanding Christ's atonement as a work of wisdom calls for an "at-one-ment" of theories of the atonement. In other words, Christ's death and resurrection are laden with implications and blessings not only for fallen humankind and the whole of creation but for our very speech and reasoning about the atonement itself. Ironically, though Christ's work is fundamentally about reconciliation, the ways we discuss this doctrine often fall short of this reality. Rather than participating in the reconciling spirit of Christ's work, our discussions of the atonement emphasize singularity (rather than plurality) and overcoming the perceived problem (rather than witnessing to the self-giving of God); they set up boundary markers and engage in biblical, doctrinal, and historical polemics.

As we will see, reappropriating the wisdom of Christ's work offers helpful resources for overcoming these divisive trends, for at-one-ing the doctrine of the atonement. The goal here, as throughout the book, is to allow the biblical witness to guide us in thinking more expansively about the fruits and implications of the death and resurrection of Christ—and to allow those truths we embrace to be enriched by the addition and incorporation of still further riches contained within our Scriptures in their manifold testimony to the abundant riches we have in Christ.

BREADTH VS. SINGULARITY

God's work is not merely creative, bringing an abundance of creatures out of nothing (*creatio ex nihilo*), but re-creative (*recreatio ex corruptio*), bringing reconciliation, salvation, and fullness of life to his fallen creation. Both of these are works of his wisdom, works in which God makes himself the means of fittingly bringing about the range of his complex purposes. Dwelling on this fact, contemplating the wisdom of God's activity, heightens our awareness and appreciation of the massive breadth of his saving work in Christ, warning against an overly narrow construal of the atonement.

One of the most important ways we slip into an overly narrow construal of the atonement is in governing imagery we choose to express our views. Look, for example, at the ten pages of endorsements at the beginning of *Pierced for*

Our Transgressions, a book written in defense of penal substitution.[1] D. A. Carson, in the first endorsement, writes: "This book is important … because it deals so competently with what lies at the heart of Christ's work." Others follow suit, describing penal substitution as the "heart of the gospel," "a central biblical truth," "the very heart of the Christian message," a doctrine of "central importance," one of the "fundamentals of the Christian faith," the "soteriological heart of historic Christianity," the "heart of [the] doctrine" of the atonement, "at the heart of the Christian faith," and so on.

But what do these comments about the centrality of the penal substitution view mean? The authors explain: "Some doctrines are more central than others *in the sense that they are more closely related to a greater number of biblical doctrines.* … Removing a central piece will … disrupt more elements of the picture [of a jigsaw puzzle] than omitting one of the corners." Furthermore, "other aspects of the atonement cease to make sense if penal substitution is denied." In this sense, "far from being *alternatives* to penal substitution," other aspects of Christ's work "are outworkings of it. As the hub from which all these other doctrines fan out, penal substitution is surely central."[2]

---

1. S. Jeffery, Michael Ovey, and Andrew Sach, *Pierced for Our Transgressions: Rediscovering the Glory of Penal Substitution* (Wheaton, IL: Crossway, 2007). To be fair, this is not a position unique to these authors. Cf., for instance, the "Forum" of *Southern Baptist Journal of Theology* 11, no. 2, and Thomas R. Schreiner, "Penal Substitution View," in *The Nature of the Atonement: Four Views*, ed. James K. Beilby and Paul R. Eddy (Downers Grove: IVP Academic, 2006). For a very helpful historical overview of this emphasis on penal substitution, see Stephen R. Holmes, "Ransomed, Healed, Restored, Forgiven: Evangelical Accounts of the Atonement," in *The Atonement Debate: Papers from the London Symposium on the Theology of Atonement*, ed. Derek Tidball, David Hilborn, and Justin Thacker (Grand Rapids: Zondervan, 2008).

2. Jeffery, Ovey, and Sach, *Pierced for Our Transgressions*, 210–11.

This is like saying that the marriage relationship is the heart or foundation of all other relationships: they are all derived from or connected to marriage in some way or other, and if we did away with the marriage relationship, all other relationships would be significantly distorted. Or we might claim that the Chinese economy is the heart of the world's economy: all other economies are derived from or connected to it, and what happens to the Chinese economy has greater consequences for other economies than any other single economy. Marriage and the Chinese economy are important, but are claims about their centrality relative to others of their kind accurate? If centrality is an accurate way of looking at things, we would do well to attend to it, but centrality may not always be the best category for understanding the issues at hand.

I want to be quite clear that I am not questioning the truth of penal substitution at all. On the contrary, I affirm it. I do not question the truth of penal substitution but rather its role in relation to other theories of the atonement.

When faced with the issue of how various theories of the atonement relate to one another, one option is to prioritize the theories or explain how one includes the others within it. Another alternative is to say that all are equally valid metaphors or attempts to explain what is ultimately beyond our capacity to explain. My approach is to root our work on theories of the atonement within the greater reality of the life of God, using that to explain why every theory has its own proper dignity. This eliminates the need to elevate one or another theory as central or more important than the others.[3]

---

3. See Johnson, *Atonement: A Guide for the Perplexed*, esp. chap. 4.

Part of the motivation for affirming the centrality of one theory stems from the influence of Aulén.[4] There is an implied order and sequence to his three theories of the atonement (exemplarist, satisfaction, and classic or *Christus Victor*). Christ is an example because he did something specific that can serve as an example. What is that thing that he did? He accomplished our salvation (via satisfaction or penal substitution), which resulted in our freedom from the power of Satan. But as we have seen, this is a flawed way of approaching the doctrine, because there are not three main theories of the doctrine of Christ's work. If we begin instead with the doctrine of God, paying particular attention to the role of the divine attributes in our theories of the atonement, the need for ordering or prioritizing the theories dissipates. The need to see one theory as central, in short, is in large part a problem unique to Aulén's unfortunate way of setting up the doctrine.

Nevertheless, "heart" language is alive and well in discussions of the doctrine, and we do well to understand its dynamics. Using this kind of language seems to have two main benefits. First, claims about the heart, centrality, or foundation draw our attention to what is most important, allowing us to develop our priorities accordingly. If, for instance, the German language were the heart of international industry, a Brazilian could prioritize her language study accordingly, choosing to take a course in German rather than French or English. Second, claims about the heart or foundation are inherently relational. They draw our attention not only to the center but also to that of which they are the center, encouraging us to draw connections between the center and the periphery, the heart and the circulatory system or other organs.

---

4. See the discussion in the introduction.

To return to an earlier example, suggesting that the Chinese economy is the heart of the world economy would motivate us to explore other economies and their relation to the Chinese economy. These are significant benefits worth appreciating. If there is in fact a heart, center, or foundation to something, we would do well to attend to it.

But there are also dangers to using this language. In spite of its power and potential, the language is ultimately inaccurate. What is the heart of a football team? The quarterback, running back, coach, general manager, fans? While calling someone the heart of a team is a great compliment, ultimately I am not sure that there is such a thing (though the media seems to disagree, having described about 10 different players or coaches as the heart of my own favorite team in the last year). If we raise the stakes, the problem is even more evident. What happens if we fabricate the "heart" of a vitally important issue such as pervasive racism, deep conflict within a church body, or a long trend of decay, corruption, and civil war in a country? The harmful consequences are potentially as powerful as the benefits.

Using fabricated "heart" language can result in either scapegoating or overprivileging. In scapegoating, we artificially isolate problems and feel as though by dealing with them we have dealt with the underlying issue. I observed this in a church where systemic patterns of sloth and complacency in the congregation encouraged the pastor and his wife to do far too much for the church. When the couple fell into temptation and sin, the congregation was content to locate the heart of its problems in this couple (that had in fact sinned). By firing them, they felt as though they had purged the community of its problems by dealing with the "heart" or "root" of the issue.

Fabricating a heart enabled the congregation to continue in its self-complacent patterns of sin that had put the couple into such a difficult place to begin with, ill-equipped to deal with temptation.

The twin sibling of scapegoating is the similarly damaging dynamic of overprivileging. Sticking with church dynamics, let's say that a church determines that the youth are the heart of the church, since they are its future (without youth growing up to become mature Christians, the ranks of church membership will dwindle and die). Such a church might lavish attention on the youth in the form of pastoral energy, finances, events, and the like. While not in and of itself a bad thing, what might be the consequences of such overprivileging? A moment's thought would suggest problems such as entitlement, ignoring people when they become older than the favored age bracket, resentment on the part of other groups in the church (such as young adults, childless couples, and the elderly), and overall inward focus as the church ignores its mission and vocation.

Both scapegoating and its brightly clad twin of overprivileging are destructive to a community in the long run. They both rely on a fabricated "heart" as the conceptual mechanism feeding the way people direct their energy and attention—the "heart of darkness and evil" and the "heart of goodness and hope." Exploring the heart of a matter is a powerful and energizing move when there is in fact a heart, but fabricating one when there is no such thing is an equally damaging move, no matter how well intentioned it might be (and the people in both of the above examples from church life were well intentioned if nothing else).

As mentioned above, pursuing a heart of the atonement will have great (if temporary and ultimately detrimental) benefits, such as the growth in excitement that comes from honing in on a single factor, the accompanying energy created by relating other factors to the main one, and even the (potentially artificial) polemic energy created by naysayers, whether of the moderate or aggressive sort. But if such a move is dangerous when there is not in fact a heart, how should we then understand the atonement?

Here the wisdom of the atonement has a decisive role to play. Attending to the fact that Christ's atoning work was a work of wisdom brings powerfully to mind the way in which God, through one simple means, brings about a massive range of purposes. The means in question is clearly the death and resurrection of the incarnate Son of God by the will of the Father and in the power of the Spirit, and the abundant range of purposes we have already seen in the previous chapter. This is where the early creeds of the church rest content, refraining from doctrinal elaboration and specification of the meaning and significance of the death and resurrection of Jesus. How does penal substitution play a role within this vision?

Certain contemporary defenses of penal substitution as the "heart of the atonement" see penal substitution as the *means* of accomplishing the work of God.[5] Without this central means, the argument goes, the whole work of Christ collapses (or at least suffers greatly). But when we see the

---

5. My interaction with certain forms of penal substitution here has to do with contemporary treatments of the doctrine. The history of this doctrine is far more nuanced. There were times when the defense of penal substitution was in fact a defense of the orthodox Christian faith, not because penal substitution itself is *the* orthodox view, but because the criticisms leveled against it attacked not merely penal substitution but the whole doctrine of the atonement.

atonement from the perspective of wisdom, we can discern several flaws in this line of reasoning. First, the general point is that the heart or foundation of the atonement is the means, not the end. Penal substitution is the heart, in this argument, because it is the means by which all else happens within the atonement. This would be somewhat akin to arguing that the heart or center of marriage is the wedding vow as opposed to a lifelong fruitful relationship of love, faithfulness, and mutual self-giving—because the vows are means by which the marriage is constituted. This would seem to reverse priorities, drawing too much attention to the means and not enough to the end.[6]

Second, while the means employed by wisdom is simple—the death and resurrection of Jesus—simplicity within the Christian faith will always be a specific kind of simplicity. This is a rich and abundant simplicity, rooted in the divine simplicity of God, in which the simplicity is an inherent unity and interweaving of a great and abundant diversity. Just as it is proper to speak of the oneness and simplicity of God, so it is proper to speak of the threeness and complexity of God; he is the triune God, one God in three persons, and he is simple as the one he is in the abundance of his divine attributes. The life, death, and resurrection of Jesus is simple in the same way—it is a single, whole work, but it is not simplistic. Clearly, Jesus is our substitute—as Isaiah 52-53 affirms, God's servant "shall act wisely" (Isa 52:13), explaining that "he has borne our griefs and carried our sorrows" (Isa 53:4); "the LORD has laid on him the iniquity of us all" (Isa 53:6) and "he bore the sin of

---

6. See arguments to this point in Graham A. Cole, *God the Peacemaker* (Downers Grove, IL: InterVarsity Press, 2009), 233-39; Gregory A. Boyd, "Christus Victor View," in *The Nature of the Atonement*, 42-45.

many" (Isa 53:12).[7] But is he not more than that? Indeed, he is also our representative, our example.[8] As Athanasius puts it, he is our image, in whom we are remade.[9] If Jesus were simply our substitute, then he would have done his work for us, in our place. And while Scripture clearly affirms this, it simultaneously affirms that Christ is our representative: the work he does, he does in such a way that we are in him. This point is made in fruitful tension with the substitutionary framework in Galatians 2:20. Paul begins by writing, "I have been crucified with Christ," which is a profoundly representational statement (I was crucified *with Christ*, rather than he was crucified *for me*). However, he concludes the sentence: "And the life I now live in the flesh I live by faith in the Son of God, who loved me and gave himself for me." This is a more substitutionary frame of reference, where God does something "for us," or "in our place, in our stead." The same logic occurs with Christ as example, specifically with regard to his revelatory work, as he makes known to us in a unique and unprecedented way the nature, will, and life of God. While Christ's work is clearly substitutionary, it is not this alone.

Third, when we see Christ's work as a work of wisdom, with our heightened sense of the multiplicity of ends brought about by Christ, we carefully attend to the role of *penalty*

---

7. It is important to distinguish between substitution generally and penal substitution. The later specifies a certain kind of substitution (a vicarious bearing of our sin, penalty, and punishment), whereas the former is more generic, allowing for Christ bearing our sin in ways which include but also transcend the bearing of penalty, such as bearing our shame, dishonor or attempts to hide from God's presence.

8. Johnson, *Atonement: A Guide for the Perplexed*, 43–46; Thomas F. Torrance, *The Mediation of Christ* (Colorado Springs: Helmers & Howard, 1992), 79–81; Steve Chalke, "The Redemption of the Cross," in *The Atonement Debate*, 37; Stephen Finlan, *Problems with Atonement: The Origins of, and Controversy About, the Atonement Doctrine* (Collegeville, MN: Liturgical Press, 2005).

9. Athanasius, *On the Incarnation*, §13–14.

within penal substitution. Is penalty at the heart of the gospel? It is certainly a valid dimension of the gospel, but what does it mean to make it the heart?[10] Essentially, if penalty or guilt is the heart of sin, then justice is the heart of God's character—for what is sin but a revolt against the character and will of God? If sin is guilt that incurs a penalty, the God against whom such sin is committed is the God of justice.

But wisdom recoils at such a point. Who are we to transition from affirming the justice of God, which Scripture demands, to giving it preeminence over his love, faithfulness, and the host of other attributes testified throughout Scripture? An emphasis on wisdom demands proper attention to the justice of God and the guilt and penalty of our sin. But in its reconciliation of all things, and its clear grasp of the way that God in his wisdom brings all things to completion in this work, it refuses to give preeminence to one of God's attributes over the others—the full spectrum of the character or attributes of God is the wellspring of wisdom's creative work. Wisdom is powerful, good, life-giving, loving, and knowledgeable precisely because it is the attribute that orchestrates the unified activity of God, unleashing the full resources of God's character upon the problem of our sin. To emphasize justice over the other aspects of God's character is to destroy the unity of God, on the one hand, and to gut the wisdom of God on the other.

To be clear, I am not placing wisdom on the throne just vacated by justice. Wisdom is no more the heart of God's character than justice is. The fact that it is an orchestrating attribute gives it no more significance within the life of God than any other attribute.

---

10. See Barth, *Church Dogmatics* IV/1, 253–54.

Finally, the emphasis on God's wisdom demands that we attend to a range of ends that are included in, but far broader than, those inherent to penal substitution. While we are in fact made innocent and just by God through the substitutionary death and resurrection of Christ, this is no more the heart or foundation of the atonement than any one country is the heart or foundation of the world. The work of Wisdom incarnate is vastly greater than the problem of our guilt, or even merely human problems. God's reconciling work is far more expansive, far more comprehensive, than this. God's atoning work includes but reaches beyond human bondage to sin, including the fate of fallen and unfallen angels, animals, and the earth itself. Penal substitution is in no way the heart of Christ's atonement, though it is without question a vital part of the work of Christ. We must make both a decisive affirmation of penal substitution as one aspect of the wise work of Wisdom incarnate and a decisive rejection of any claims to its primacy or centrality. Wisdom will not sacrifice the whole for a part, exchanging the genuine treasure of God for whole kingdoms and worlds of other goods.

The problem of making one theory of the atonement into the "heart" is not unique to adherents of penal substitution. Wisdom is and always will be embattled by opponents who tempt it with goods rightfully its own, opponents who offer the part in exchange for the whole, creating conflict, dissolution, and jealousy where there need be none. At every turn we are tempted to make one good thing preeminent over others, distorting the whole in order to make our small portion all the more secure or valuable. Consequently, we take the modest good touted by another as a threat to the goods we ourselves hold dear. In doing this, we continue to rip and tear the garments of Boethius' Lady Philosophy, treasuring them as our own, resenting the treasures of others. We refuse to acknowledge the resounding and triumphant proclamation of Wisdom calling out in the streets, offering a comprehensive and total possession of the full range of goods that the good and wise God offers us in Christ through the fulfillment of creation itself. We turn our backs on an abundance and worlds upon worlds of goods, which we have not by possession but by participation in and with God as his wise children. Too often we fight, not for too much, not for something too precious, but for something not good enough, not comprehensive enough, not precious enough.[11]

The alternative to our miserly scrambling, our haste, our jealousy, our petty squabbles, is no weak affirmation of tolerance, peace, or the like. It can be no well-meant affirmation of riches and diversity. Scot McKnight, Mark Baker, and Joel Green (among others) have advanced accounts of the atonement that refer to an abundance of theories, explanations, or metaphors for the work of Christ, using such images as a bag of golf clubs or a kaleidoscope. While this is an improvement, I question whether they have provided a sufficiently theological framework for making sense of this diversity, which in turn would equip us to use it responsibly in theological, homiletic, and pastoral contexts.[12] The question is: what funds this diversity? The premise of the present work, developed at length in *Atonement: A Guide for the Perplexed*, is that nothing but the diversity proper to the life of the triune God in the

---

11. I owe this insight to C. S. Lewis, "The Weight of Glory," in *Screwtape Proposes a Toast and Other Pieces* (Glasgow: Collins, 1985).

12. McKnight, *Community*; Baker and Green, *Recovering*; Green, "Kaleidoscopic View. " For my fuller account of these matters, see chaps. 1–4 of Johnson, *Atonement: A Guide for the Perplexed*.

fullness of his divine attributes will account for the diversity inherent within the doctrine of Christ's saving work.

So in the place of both heart language and variety language, I propose that we speak of the irreducible complexity of the work of Christ. I am here borrowing a concept often used in Christian apologetics—the argument for the intelligent design of biological systems given that they are complex in a way that they will not function if only some of the parts work. A traditional mousetrap, for example, is irreducibly complex; it consists of a number of parts, each of which must be fully functioning for the trap to work. Each of the parts is essential in that the absence of any one of them will result in the failure of the trap to function. The "heart" of the mousetrap consists of the irreducibly complex combination of parts. The same is true of the atonement: penal substitution is one of the many parts that must be present for God's atoning work to be complete—but only one among a host of others.

This brings us to the divine wisdom, the living, powerful and active wisdom of God, who holds his creation dear to his heart, making himself in his abundant diversity the means to accomplishing the end of his glorious and abundant purposes. Only in him, only in his wisdom, do we have the resources and vision to participate in this massive and comprehensive work of reconciliation. Only in him do we have the wisdom not only to critique but to embrace, not only to speak but to listen, not only tear down but to build up, not only to be defensive but to open our gates in confidence, not to quarantine but to heal, not to entrench but to disarm. Only the wisdom of God enacted in Christ frees us to bring reconciliation where there is conflict—a claim as true of theories of the atonement as it is of the guilty, shamed, and groaning creatures and creation of which they speak.

Boundary Markers

My sense is that the "heart," "center," and "foundation" language used in so many discussions of the atonement is primarily a matter of boundary markers. In other words, this is not a claim about what is the "heart" and what is the "brain" or "lungs," and neither is it a matter of securing foundational elements so as to go on to explore others. Rather, talk about the "heart" of the atonement is a way of defending a certain way of doing theology by artificially establishing penal substitution (for example) as the litmus test or "shibboleth" (Judg 12:5–7) of orthodoxy. Those who develop nonviolent theories of the atonement are setting up boundary markers just as aggressively as defenders of penal substitution; the goal is to establish a test, or defensive mechanism, to safeguard the theological task, whether that is a deeply biblical ethical safeguard from dangerous and unbiblical behavior or an equally biblical theological safeguard from dangerous and unbiblical thinking that is insufficiently Trinitarian and Christological.

However, boundary markers are not inherently evil. They play a vital role in theology, not to mention everyday life. In the introduction to *The Atonement Debate*, David Hilborn carefully and graciously sets the stage in terms of boundary markers, the goal of which is:

> ... prompt consideration of the extent to which penal substitution ought to define the limits of evangelical orthodoxy, whether it should function for evangelicals as a "centered" or

> a "bounded" set. Yet alongside all the key ex-
> egetical and theological work which appears
> in this book, these further ecclesiological and
> relational issues warrant close attention, lest
> the division which has plagued evangelical
> life and mission in the past be too heedlessly
> championed and that same gospel ministry be
> hampered.[13]

The question of what defines a denomination, evangelical theology, or a political party is valid and needful; it helps establish identity and boundaries. These not only keep out threatening forces but provide a fixed reference from which to live and move when outside the boundaries, much as a family culture and identity provide the wellspring for action and decision-making on the part of children when they are away from home. But because these matters are so important, we need to take exceptional care which markers we choose. While "good fences make good neighbors,"[14] a poorly chosen boundary makes for confusion and conflict in years to come.

But approaching the atonement via wisdom offers us resources for thinking about theological boundary markers. For what is a boundary marker but a strategy, a means developed to secure a certain end, and therefore an attempt at wisdom? Boundary-marker thinking argues that the best way, the wise way, to do theology is by staking out certain ground and claiming it as our own so we can defend ourselves from

---

13. Tidball, Hilborn, and Thacker, eds., *The Atonement Debate*, 28.
14. Robert Frost, "Mending Wall," in *The Complete Poems of Robert Frost: Complete and Unabridged* (New York: Macmillan, 2002), 33–34.

corruption and attack.[15] How does Wisdom's atoning work inform the wisdom of such a strategy?

First, the wisdom of God is not primarily passive or defensive. The wisdom of God is above all active and powerful. While there is a place in God's wisdom for defensive strategies, this is not his primary mode of action. God, in his wisdom, became man and dwelt among us. His was an invasive strategy, a lovingly aggressive move in which Wisdom enters the city of Dis, the kingdom of folly from Dante's *Inferno*. Neither God in his wisdom nor his people as they share in it are to think primarily in terms of boundaries, safety, or defense from attack. The way of God's wisdom is far more powerful, far more creative than that; it is able to honor the need for safety and boundaries within a larger and more constructive frame of reference.

This emphasis on invasion need not be triumphalist, however. In fact, it must not be so, for the way of wisdom is the way of suffering, of death. The ever-wise God dealt with his enemies, his opponents, by dying for them. This is the way of wisdom in which we are to walk. We are to view the enemy not as an enemy but as an alienated and even hostile sibling whom we go to great lengths to love. In the academy, in theological discourse, wisdom is just as much a matter of suffering, of losing face, of feeling pain and loss, as it was for Christ (even if it is not a matter of our own sin, pride, and folly, which is all too often the case). This suffering might take various forms, from the pain of revisiting treasured convictions to the powerful social losses incurred by refusing to toe the party line in the

---

15. For those looking to better understand this notion of a boundary marker, I commend the distinction between bounded-set thinking and centered-set thinking such as one finds developed in the work of missiologist Paul Hiebert.

goal of seeking reconciliation between camps.[16] It certainly means honoring and embracing the valid insights of our interlocutors, not to mention embracing the opportunity to find ourselves in the wrong and be corrected—virtues as needed in marriage and civil service as in the academy.

But ours is not a blind or purposeless suffering, as though suffering were good for its own sake. This is a suffering for the sake of something greater, more powerful, and more effective for reconciliation. We meditate upon the saving work of Wisdom, speaking and writing on the subject, not to strengthen weak arguments, not to defend a challenged worldview, and not in compliance with social pressures (whether they are conservative or liberal, they are just as blinding and constraining). Rather, we contemplate and share out of the sheer joy of participating in the work of the ever-wise God, of Wisdom incarnate. The theological task, in other words, is

---

16. In this we catch a glimpse of the mutually informing nature of the intellectual virtues through the relationship between wisdom and courage. As Roberts and Wood put it, "Intellectual *courage* is an ability to perform intellectual tasks well despite what one takes to be significant threats. The threats may be such things as loss of employment or other opportunities, loss of reputation or status, loss of home or friends, even bodily harm or loss of life" (Roberts and Wood, *Intellectual Virtues*, 76). Wisdom plays an immense role in this, discerning whether the task is worth pursuing despite the threat and the best way to pursue it amidst that threat. Roberts and Wood describe this as the "interdependence" of the virtues, in which a picture emerges "of a character fitted, capacitated, attuned, and oriented in a variety of ways for a variety of life situations and activities in those situations, such that the possessor of that character lives well" (ibid., 80). Cf. the similar claim of Timpe and Boyd concerning the "Interconnection Claim" in which there is a "probabilistic correlation between having one virtue and having the other virtues" (Timpe and Boyd, *Virtues and Their Vices*, 7). Further on, Roberts and Wood suggest that "each of the virtues has its own department of practical wisdom: firmness, courage, humility, autonomy, and generosity each has its own patterns of deliberation (non-deliberation) and perception (non-perception)—terms in which the agent thinks about and sees the situations of his epistemic life, and all this cognition is aimed at the epistemic goods" (Roberts and Wood, *Intellectual Virtues*, 311).

done in joy and confidence because it is a participation in the powerful and effective wisdom of God.

To participate in God's wisdom is to participate in his reconciling project, since God's action in Christ teaches us that wisdom is a reconciling reality. It is the human virtue and the divine attribute by which we discern the fitting means for bringing about the reconciliation and fulfillment of all things. Wisdom, then, is not generic strategizing or scheming. In fact, wisdom opposes scheming in the sense of "finding a way around things"—a subtle way of getting what you want. Portuguese is blessed with a singularly felicitous word for such scheming: *jeitinho*. The word, which defies definition apart from a certain contortion of the face and shrug of the shoulders, means "a little way around things." The opposite of such a concept is Edwards' "glorious contrivance."[17] Instead of scheming, wisdom is inherently ordered toward reconciliation. Think, for instance, of the radical differences between the nature of wisdom portrayed in the Greek hero Odysseus, the master of craft and resources, and the work of Wisdom incarnate.

What then does it mean to venture into atonement debates? Not to win. Not to overpower. Not to show others to be wrong. Not to critique. The goal in atonement debates is above all to participate in the reconciliation of divine Wisdom, a matter just as true of our theories as it is of our lives. Wisdom-saturated debates aimed at reconciliation are characterized by a longing to learn from the other, whether that be gaining new insights or finding yet richer ways of understanding familiar material. In them, we are eager to use the other as an occasion for revisiting and re-questioning our convictions,

17. Edwards, "The Wisdom of God Displayed in the Way of Salvation," 156.

embracing critique as an opportunity to thankfully discard bad arguments, purifying our complex and muddled convictions, and humbly repenting of our sin, of the unintentional consequences of our thinking, or of our biases. In such debates, we have a jealous longing to build up our neighbor, affirming wherever possible the methodological, contextual, conceptual, or applicational moves they make. We have a resounding confidence, joy, and humility stemming from participating in a reality greater than ourselves, and therefore one in which we are not threatened by our own failures or swollen by our successes. We display a spirit of embracing or even (noncompetitively) outdoing the other at precisely that which they treasure, so that they are surprised to find the things they hold most dear in the works of their perceived opponents.

Does all this mean that wisdom is only positive and constructive? Is there no room for critique and conflict?[18] Indeed there is, for while the power of wisdom is the power of the resurrection and reconciliation, there is also wisdom in the life of Christ, including his conflict with the leaders of Israel. Wisdom, though positive and constructive, embraces the way of suffering and the cross, all in the joyful shadow of the resurrection. Wisdom embraces conflict as a sure means toward fulfillment and reconciliation, for to avoid it is to take a circuitous and ultimately unmanageable path that is sure to get us hopelessly lost.

What does wise conflict look like? First, the end of conflict is reconciliation, just as the goal of separation and divorce is remarriage, the purpose of civil war is the well being of the

---

18. Consider, for instance, the twin proverbs of Prov 26:4–5: "Answer not a fool according to his folly, lest you be like him yourself. Answer a fool according to his folly, lest he be wise in his own eyes."

nation, the end of a fight is an embrace. Wisdom allows for no mere triumph and no empty defeat. Life is no game with winners and losers—such a victory is too paltry a goal. When I defeat my wife in verbal conflict, I find myself the more wounded. As James puts it, "the wisdom from above is first pure, then peaceable, gentle, open to reason, full of mercy and good fruits, impartial and sincere. And a harvest of righteousness"—and, we might add, reconciliation—"is sown in peace by those who make peace" (Jas 3:17–18).

Second, we engage in conflict with all our hearts, but hearts filled with grief. While the Riders of Rohan in *The Lord of the Rings* could sing "while they slew, for the joy of battle was upon them,"[19] no such option is available to us. As fellow creatures brought into being by divine Wisdom, any conflict is intramural, conflict between brothers and sisters. Others may be deeply and powerfully wrong (as may we), and their beliefs may require firm and powerful rejoinders—but these rejoinders are aimed at helping rather than defeating, reconciling rather than terminating, and suffering alongside our siblings in the consequences of their folly and our own. Inasmuch as we enter into conflict, we do so with the weight of care and grief, longing not for victory but reconciliation. Wise conflict is a whole-hearted, attentive, and strategic rebuttal, continually seeking reconciliation and always eager to recognize both fault and insight on both sides. This is so because wisdom is powerful and effective, carefully choosing the best means to bring about the reconciliation of all things.

In debates on the doctrine of the atonement, such an attitude should deeply pervade our approach to those accounts with which we disagree. Whether we are encountering

---

19. J. R. R. Tolkien, *The Lord of the Rings* (Boston: Houghton Mifflin, 2004), 838.

feminist or womanist theologies with their powerful critiques of abuse, Girardian developments rooted largely in anthropological studies of classic texts, or the works of classic theological villains such as Peter Abelard, Faustus Socinus, or Friedrich Schleiermacher and classical biblical scholars such as Rudolf Bultmann and C. H. Dodd, we must strive for wisdom and understanding. We must seek to learn and grow through their insights first and their mistakes second. Only at the end of this process, and for the sake or reconciliation and growth, do we move on to gracious and nurturing critique. Should we take the path oft traveled, we run the risk of answering these supposed fools according to their folly, making ourselves more like them in the process (Prov 26:4).

CHAPTER 8

The Way Forward: A New Definition

The way forward in our attempt to understand the atonement, to paraphrase Robert Frost, is to embrace the fact that we have miles to go before we rest on this path of divine wisdom.[1] Understanding the atonement as a work of divine wisdom gives us access to an epic picture that binds together God's creative and re-creative enterprise, as both were accomplished by the same agent, the same means: Wisdom himself. Such a vast picture equips us in our task in three ways.

First, this picture provides the underlying logic for a plenitude of insights into the abundant and varied work of Christ. The atonement of Jesus Christ is such a vast and comprehensive work that neither the angels nor we will exhaust it. We should not expect unanimity but instead embrace the diversity of voices that together form a choir with a rich abundance of attuned and united voices expounding

---

1. Robert Frost, "Stopping by Woods on a Snowy Evening."

the manifold work of Christ. It is not a cacophony, but a choir praising a rich and varied yet simple salvation by a God who is likewise rich and varied, yet one. The diversity proper to the life of God, incarnate among us in and through the Wisdom of God, is effective to bring about the diverse abundance of God's purposes. To appreciate this range of diversity upon diversity, a host of interpreters and worshippers is necessary. The key here is to allow the death and resurrection of Jesus Christ as an event within the life of the triune God to stand as the core event of the doctrine, which we then unpack and explain in relation to the various aspects of the character of God and the dimensions of sin that these bring to light.

Second, the content of the picture impels us toward reconciliation. The means and the end are one in the person of Wisdom, together demanding, equipping, and encouraging our use of the wisdom we have in Christ toward the work of reconciliation. The atonement as a work of wisdom opens the door to an expansive project of appreciating the manifold ends accomplished by the manifold wisdom of God. To be sure, atonement as a work of wisdom is not the final word on the matter. It is not the master theory to which all others submit. But it is one of many different and warranted vantage points for understanding the work of Christ, and one that is particularly suited for energizing and helping us appreciate the full range of aspects and implications of this greatest of events, God's re-creative activity in the death and resurrection of Jesus Christ. And we, as his people, share in this mission—the mission of enacting wisdom to bring about the reconciliation of all things.

Finally, in this account we have the resources of a new and fuller definition of human wisdom. We found in chapter

4 that wisdom was a matter of living well, of *bringing about the full range of our purposes by the most fitting means, taking full account of the whole array of circumstances and factors surrounding us.* Wisdom is indeed a matter of living well, but many conflicting accounts of wisdom would agree with such a generic description. But virtues need not be—in fact, cannot be—generic, since they depend on our "conceptions of the human person and his place in the universe."[2] Depending on the different construals of the metaphysical and theological matters presupposed in those construals, they "yield strikingly different pictures of proper human functioning, and thus of the virtues."[3] Put differently, "If practical wisdom is right reason directed to the excellent human life, we can expect variations in the analyses of practical wisdom to arise out of contrasting accounts of human nature and contrasting visions of the good life."[4]

Given the unique presentation of God and his wisdom manifest in Christ's death and resurrection, we can now advance a more complete definition of wisdom in light of the work of Christ.[5] The first thing to note is that wisdom must derive its identity from God. While wisdom pertains to every action under the sun, it demands that we order these actions properly toward the origin and source of all wisdom—for "the purpose of the pursuit of wisdom is to uncover how things are ordered in relation to each other, not simply in their existence

---

2. Roberts and Wood, *Intellectual Virtues*, 22–23.

3. Ibid., 7.

4. Ibid., 38.

5. According to Richard S. Briggs, Christian wisdom is "the ability to see the world as God would have us see it" (Briggs, *Reading the Bible Wisely: An Introduction to Taking Scripture Seriously*, rev. ed. [Grand Rapids: Baker Academic, 2011], 138). Kevin Vanhoozer elaborates, "This is what the canon, the church's Scripture and the Christian's script, ultimately provides: *the ability to make judgments about the true, the good, and the beautiful that are fit 'in Christ'* " (Vanhoozer, *Drama*, 308).

but in their fullness, as God is ordered in his fullness"—and creaturely fullness occurs only within the ordering and fullness of God.[6]

Second, Christ's work specifies wisdom as an inherently communal, relational, and ultimately cosmic matter, binding together the whole of creation with its Creator. There is a place for wisdom for daily life, wisdom for business practice, wisdom for accomplishing life as we want it—a whole book is devoted to such matters in Scripture. But Christ's wisdom revealed and enacted for us on the cross and in the resurrection demands that in our pursuit of wisdom we not reduce it to a matter of personal, familial, or national strategy. Wisdom, and the ends, means, and circumstances it binds together, is cosmic in perspective, rooted in the divine life.

Third, wisdom is a matter of living well, but it should be further specified as living well with the aim of the reconciliation and fulfillment of all things. Wisdom, in other words, is a matter of living well by participating in the bringing about of the full range of God's purposes for his treasured yet fallen creation, seeking the reconciliation and fulfillment of all things. Wisdom aims not at personal success, not at national well-being, but at reconciliation—not a partial, ambiguous, or demonic reconciliation (many such exist), but a true and flourishing reconciliation rooted in the fulfillment of all things in relation to their Creator. After the pattern of our Maker and Savior, wisdom lives well by seeking the reconciliation of all things specifically through our self-involvement, which often takes the form of suffering in the power of the risen Lord. Wisdom is a self-involving, self-giving form of activity aimed at reconciliation.

---

6. Hardy, "The Grace of God and Earthly Wisdom," 233.

True wisdom is still a matter of living well, still a matter of seeking to bring about the full range of our purposes by the most fitting means, taking full account of the whole array of circumstances and factors surrounding us. It still bears on smaller, more down-to-earth concerns. But it does this in a specific way, separating it from the many perverse, abridged, or adulterated versions of wisdom that surround us now as they did in the time of Paul (1 Cor 3:18–20): ordering all of life around one's marriage and family, making decisions based on the accumulation of power, making economic policies founded on the prioritization of one's national economy over that of adjacent nations, employing the powers of evil to bring about genuine good, to name just a few. The world is full of strategies and visions that seem internally consistent and effective, yet ultimately distort, misshape, and pervert God's creative purposes, unleashing strife, chaos, and pain—sometimes immediately, and sometimes for the generations to come.

In short, true wisdom, wisdom rooted in the Wisdom of God, is a matter of seeking the full range of God's purposes for the whole of his creation by means of our self-involvement and self-giving, which often involves suffering. This takes the shape of pursuing the reconciliation of all things in and through God. And this, as we have seen, is a reality that bears just as much on our discussions of the atonement as it does upon the hosts of folly's acts and consequences surrounding us in daily life.

CHAPTER 9

Conclusion

Wisdom language permeates our Scriptures. It was there at the beginning as God created (John 1:1–3), and was there when we fell (Gen 3:6). It is a vital part of the Old Testament (Deut 4:6) and woven deeply into Hebrew thinking (not least in Proverbs). It is just as important to the New Testament and the vision Paul has for the church, the life of the Christian, and the life of Christ as a teacher and sage. All of this is rooted in the biblical account of the ever-wise God: the one who in himself is wise, and therefore creates and saves us in that same wisdom that is a vital and essential aspect of the life of God as Father, Son, and Holy Spirit.

In this book I have sketched the role of wisdom throughout the Bible, drawing on the history of theology to explore the ways that the atoning work of Christ is a work of wisdom—or more specifically, a work done by Wisdom incarnate. It is a work *of* wisdom, in which Christ for our sake bears our folly and its consequences, and a work *for* wisdom, establishing God's creatures in lives of wisdom through their participation in the life of the wise God. The result of such an approach, it turns out, is an exceptionally broad understanding of the work of Christ, because Wisdom's work of reconciliation is just as expansive as Wisdom's work of creation. Therefore it touches on every aspect of God's good creation as he seeks to make his creation "very good" in the face of our sin and folly, just as he once made it very good in a garden long ago.

This way of telling the doctrine is not preeminent over other theories, since God is no more wise than he is just, loving, omniscient, or patient. But because he is wise, and salvation is the work of his wisdom, it is a necessary and powerful aspect of the work of Christ that we would do well to contemplate and teach. And while every biblical way of exploring this doctrine—every theory of the atonement—has its insights, benefits, and implications, the unique advantage of this approach is that it shows just how expansive or comprehensive is the work of Christ. It affects not only our own status before God as individual sinners but takes into account the whole of creation, ranging from angels and ants to demons and the earth on which we walk.

And because the wisdom of God is never unaccompanied by his power, because God is the living and active God who became man for our sake and for our salvation, his work is never without its benefits. Good theology is never devoid of application. One of these benefits, one of these applications, is a renewed appreciation of the destructive power of foolishness. We must not turn a blind eye to folly. We must have as great a concern for the fool walking toward the house of Lady Folly as we find in Proverbs. To do this, we must be a people, a church, that offers more than mere platitudes and wise sayings from days gone by (again remembering the Calormenes in C. S. Lewis' *The Horse and His Boy*). We must be a people of deep and abiding wisdom.

To do this, we need to be rooted in a deep and sustaining picture of wisdom that not only finds ways to bring about our goals but also reshapes and reforms the goals we have, the means we use, and the circumstances in which we perceive ourselves to act within God's work of reconciling all things to him. What we need is "God's Wisdom *transform[ing]* human beings ... as awakening, enlightenment, revelation, when ultimate truth and value are concretely disclosed" through Christ.[1]

To be sure, this is a demanding and rewarding goal that cannot be met by following simple lessons or passing along proverbs. This is a matter of thorough enculturation that includes discipling, passing along a heritage, and training in patterns of thought and action over the course of a lifetime. But this, of course, is why Wisdom came and dwelt among us: to take upon himself our folly that we might lives of wisdom in the power of his resurrection. And this means that we, like our Lord, will seek to bring about reconciliation wherever possible, through the wisdom we have in Christ. We, like our ever-wise Lord, will seek to be peacemakers. We must make peace in ourselves and in others:

> In both cases this is the result of setting in due order those things in which peace is established, for *peace is the tranquility of order*, according to Augustine (*De Civ. Dei* xix. 13). Now it belongs to wisdom to set things in order, as the Philosopher declares (*Metaph.* i.2): wherefore peaceableness is fittingly ascribed to wisdom. The reward is expressed in the words, *they shall*

---

1. Hodgson, *God's Wisdom*, 110.

be called the children of God. Now men are called
the children of God in so far as they participate
in the likeness of the only begotten and natural
Son of God, according to Rom. 8:29, *Whom He
foreknew ... to be made conformable to the image of
His Son, Who* is Wisdom Begotten. Hence by participation in the gift of wisdom, man attains to
the sonship of God.[2]

---

2. Thomas Aquinas, *Summa Theologiæ* II–II.45.6.

Five Questions to Ask Ourselves

This book seeks to explore the life, death, and resurrection of Jesus Christ as a work of wisdom. But it also seeks to help encourage the people of God to inhabit this reality, to abandon the way of folly our Lord trod for us, and to live a life of wisdom through our participation in him. In this appendix, I offer a first step in this direction by offering five questions that stem from the above consideration of wisdom.

True wisdom, wisdom rooted in the Wisdom of God, is a matter of seeking the full range of God's purposes for the whole of his creation by means of our self-involvement and self-giving (often involving suffering), which takes the shape of pursuing the reconciliation of all things in and through God. Accordingly, we should ask ourselves these questions, which I hope might be the beginning of, or a further encouragement toward, a participation in the life of wisdom God calls us to in his Son, Wisdom incarnate:

1. **What range of purposes am I actively seeking in my life, and how does Christ's atoning work call me to revise or expand this list?**

Do the goals of my life revolve around myself, my family, my community, my nation? The purposes of Christ extended from the most downtrodden individual to the angels in the heavens. Nothing less than God's whole creative project was at stake, and we, as his children, are called by Christ's atonement to find our own lives, hurts, and ambitions within the greater picture of God's creative purposes. And we should ask this question all the more in the midst of pain, hurt, and suffering, when our goals are cut down to just one or two: health, the well-being of a child, or keeping a marriage intact.

2. **What are the circumstances I consider as I seek to navigate life with wisdom, and how does Christ's atoning work call me to revise or expand these circumstances?**

Who do we picture observing or being affected by our actions? Do we save to buy a big-screen TV, or do we save to offer an inheritance to our grandchildren? Do we think of our national government in terms of our benefits or those we can extend to immigrants? Christ's atonement concerns not merely Jesus, not the individual or community, not even God's people, but all of these and more within the sphere of all

God's creation. Christ's atoning work was a matter of God triumphing over the powers opposing him so that all of creation could witness the saving benefits of his Son's work. Our own lives have meaning and purpose within this theater, within this vast scope of circumstances that far transcend (but still include) our particular fears, pains, and concerns. Our pains are real: as we struggle with questions of sexual identity, disappointment from trusted mentors and friends, or large-scale corruption within a business, we do indeed suffer. But we suffer within a bigger picture, consumed by the death and resurrection of Christ, which puts all things in perspective.

3. **What are the means I employ in my attempt to live wisely, and how does Christ's making himself the means of bringing about his purposes challenge me in the means that I employ?**

How do we make things happen? Do we use time that rightfully belongs to our children to advance ourselves at work? Do we throw colleagues under the bus in an effort to advance ourselves? Do we overwhelm interlocutors in defense of the truth we so clearly see? Life is full of pain and hurt—both our own and that of those we love—that we desperately long to overcome. But how do we accomplish this? The way of wisdom trod by our Lord was a particular

form of wisdom, a particular form of overcoming evil not simply by power, not simply
by scheming and strategy, but by means of triumphant wisdom involving both self-sacrifice
and resurrection.

4. **How can I involve myself in the pain of
   others so that I might follow Jesus in the
   way of self-sacrifice in order to bring about
   a genuine and long-lasting transformation
   and reconciliation in the lives of others?**

Gifts, material abundance, and other tokens of
power may in fact have some significant blessing to bestow. Yet the way of God in his wisdom
was a self-investing form of self-sacrifice in
which God made himself the means of bringing
about his own goals, made himself the means in
his self-sacrifice. How can we follow this path,
investing our lives in the lives and needs of others, so that our own suffering and loss might be
to their great joy and benefit?

Lest the fourth question lead to a disastrous and impossible
life of self-sacrifice, we must ask a final and most important question.

5. **How can I involve myself self-sacrificially
   in the lives of others, *in the power of the
   risen Lord*?**

We are free to sacrifice ourselves, free to give
ourselves up, free to take on the burdens and

pains of our neighbors, not because we are insignificant, not as a form of punishment or penance, not because this is demanded by a Lord who cares little for us, but because we are a people who live in the power of the resurrection. We are motivated, carried, and empowered by a living hope that exudes the vitality, power, and reality of the resurrection. This is not a hopeless, bitter self-sacrifice in which our death prolongs the life of another in misery. This is the power of the risen Lord, and therefore a power that allows us to descend into hurt through the ascent and nourishment we already taste as his children.

BIBLIOGRAPHY

Athanasius. *On the Incarnation.* Translated by John Behr. Yonkers, NY: St. Vladimir's Seminary Press, 2011.

Aulén, Gustaf. *Christus Victor: An Historical Study of the Three Main Types of the Idea of Atonement.* Translated by A. G. Hebert. New York: Macmillan, 1951.

Baker, Mark D., and Joel B. Green. *Recovering the Scandal of the Cross: Atonement in New Testament and Contemporary Contexts.* Downers Grove, IL: InterVarsity Press, 2003.

Barth, Karl. "The Beginning of Wisdom." In *Deliverance to the Captives.* New York: Harper & Row, 1961.

———. *The Doctrine of God.* Vol. 2, pt. 1 of *Church Dogmatics.* Edited by G. W. Bromiley and T. F. Torrance. Edinburgh: T&T Clark, 1980.

———. *The Doctrine of Reconciliation.* Vol. 4, pt. 1 of *Church Dogmatics.* Edited by G. W. Bromiley and T. F. Torrance. Edinburgh: T&T Clark, 1988.

———. *Dogmatics in Outline.* Translated by G. T. Thompson. New York: Harper, 1959.

Boethius. *The Consolation of Philosophy.* Translated by V. E. Watts. New York: Penguin, 1999.

Boyd, Gregory A. "Christus Victor View." In *The Nature of the Atonement: Four Views,* edited by James K. Beilby and Paul R. Eddy, 23-49. Downers Grove, IL: IVP Academic, 2006.

Briggs, Richard S. *Reading the Bible Wisely: An Introduction to Taking Scripture Seriously.* Rev. ed. Grand Rapids: Baker Academic, 2011.

Chalke, Steve. "The Redemption of the Cross." In *The Atonement Debate: Papers from the London Symposium on the Theology of Atonement,* edited by Derek Tidball, David Hilborn, and Justin Thacker. Grand Rapids: Zondervan, 2008.

Charry, Ellen T. *By the Renewing of Your Minds: The Pastoral Function of Christian Doctrine*. New York: Oxford University Press, 1997.

Chaucer, Geoffrey. *The Canterbury Tales*. Translated by Nevill Coghill. New York: Penguin, 2003.

Cole, Graham A. *God the Peacemaker*. Downers Grove, IL: InterVarsity Press, 2009.

Edwards, Jonathan. "The Wisdom of God Displayed in the Way of Salvation." In *The Works of Jonathan Edwards*, edited by Henry Rogers, Sereno Edwards Dwight, and Edward Hickman. Peabody, MA: Hendrickson, 1998.

Finlan, Stephen. *Problems with Atonement: The Origins of, and Controversy About, the Atonement Doctrine*. Collegeville, MN: Liturgical Press, 2005.

Ford, David. *Theology: A Very Short Introduction*. New York: Oxford University Press, 2000.

"Forum: The Atonement Under Fire." *Southern Baptist Journal of Theology* 11, no. 2 (Summer 2007): 104–114.

Frost, Robert. "Mending Wall." In *The Complete Poems of Robert Frost: Complete and Unabridged*. New York: Macmillan, 2002.

Gathercole, Simon J. *The Preexistent Son: Recovering the Christologies of Matthew, Mark, and Luke*. Grand Rapids: Eerdmans, 2006.

Graham, Gordon. "Atonement." In *The Cambridge Companion to Christian Philosophical Theology*, edited by Charles Taliaferro and Chad V. Meister, 124–35. New York: Cambridge University Press, 2010.

Green, Joel B. "Kaleidoscopic View." In *The Nature of the Atonement: Four Views*, edited by James K. Beilby and Paul R. Eddy, 157–85. Downers Grove, IL: IVP Academic, 2006.

Gregory of Nyssa. "An Address on Religious Instruction." In *Christology of the Later Fathers*, edited by Edward R. Hardy, 268–326. Philadelphia: Westminster, 1954.

Gunton, Colin E. *The Actuality of Atonement: A Study of Metaphor, Rationality, and the Christian Tradition*. Grand Rapids: Eerdmans, 1989.

Hamilton, S. Mark. "Jonathan Edwards, Anselmic Satisfaction and God's Moral Government." *International Journal of Systematic Theology* 17 no. 1 (2015): 46–67.

Hardy, Daniel W. "The Grace of God and Earthly Wisdom." In *Where Shall Wisdom Be Found? Wisdom in the Bible, the Church, and the Contemporary World*, edited by Stephen C. Barton, 231–48. Edinburgh: T&T Clark, 1999.

Herbert, George. "Death." In *The Works of George Herbert*. London: George Routledge, 1853.

Hodgson, Peter Crafts. *God's Wisdom: Toward a Theology of Education.* Louisville: Westminster John Knox, 1999.

Holmes, Stephen R. "A Simple Salvation? Soteriology and the Perfections of God." In *God of Salvation: Soteriology in Theological Perspective*, edited by Ivor J. Davidson and Murray A. Rae, 35–46. Burlington, VT: Ashgate, 2011.

———. "Ransomed, Healed, Restored, Forgiven: Evangelical Accounts of the Atonement." In *The Atonement Debate: Papers from the London Symposium on the Theology of Atonement,* edited by Derek Tidball, David Hilborn, and Justin Thacker. Grand Rapids: Zondervan, 2008.

Irenaeus. "Against Heresies." In *The Ante-Nicene Fathers*, edited by Alexander Roberts and James Donaldson. Peabody, MA: Hendrickson, 2004.

———. *On the Apostolic Preaching.* Translated by John Behr. Crestwood, NY: St. Vladimir's Seminary Press, 1997.

Jeffery, S., Michael Ovey, and Andrew Sach. *Pierced for Our Transgressions: Rediscovering the Glory of Penal Substitution.* Wheaton, IL: Crossway, 2007.

John of the Cross. *The Collected Works of St. John of the Cross.* Washington, DC: Institute of Carmelite Studies, 1979.

Johnson, Adam. "A Fuller Account: The Role of 'Fittingness' in Thomas Aquinas' Development of the Doctrine of the Atonement." *International Journal of Systematic Theology* 12, no. 3 (2010): 302–18.

———. *Atonement: A Guide for the Perplexed.* New York: T&T Clark, 2015.

————. *God's Being in Reconciliation: The Theological Basis of the Unity and Diversity of the Atonement in the Theology of Karl Barth.* New York: T&T Clark, 2012.

Johnson, Adam, and Kyle Strobel. "Atoning Wisdom: The Wisdom of God in the Way of Salvation." In *Locating Atonement*, edited by Oliver Crisp and Fred Sanders. Grand Rapids: Zondervan, 2015.

Kamtekar, Rachana. "Ancient Virtue Ethics: An Overview with an Emphasis on Practical Wisdom." In *The Cambridge Companion to Virtue Ethics*, edited by Daniel C. Russell, 29–48. New York: Cambridge University Press, 2013.

Kant, Immanuel. *Religion within the Boundaries of Mere Reason.* Translated by Allen W. Wood and George Di Giovanni. New York: Cambridge University Press, 1998.

Lewis, C. S. "The Weight of Glory." In *Screwtape Proposes a Toast and Other Pieces.* Glasgow: Collins, 1985.

————. *The Magician's Nephew.* New York: Macmillan, 1964.

Lombardo, Nicholas E. *The Father's Will: Christ's Crucifixion and the Goodness of God.* New York: Oxford University Press, 2013.

Marcus Aurelius. *Meditations.* Translated by Robin Hard. New York: Oxford University Press, 2011.

McKnight, Scot. *A Community Called Atonement.* Nashville: Abingdon, 2007.

McPhee, John. "Omission: Choosing What to Leave Out." *New Yorker*, September 14, 2015. http://www.newyorker.com/magazine/2015/09/14/omission

Minns, Denis. *Irenaeus: An Introduction.* New York: T&T Clark, 2010.

Packer, J. I. *Knowing God.* Downers Grove, IL: InterVarsity Press, 1993.

Plato. "Apology." In *Complete Works.* Edited by John M. Cooper. Indianapolis: Hackett, 1997.

Pseudo-Dionysius. *The Complete Works.* Translated by Colm Luibheid. New York: Paulist Press, 1987.

Roberts, Robert Campbell, and W. Jay Wood. *Intellectual Virtues: An Essay in Regulative Epistemology.* New York: Oxford University Press, 2007.

Schleiermacher, Friedrich. *The Christian Faith.* Edinburgh: T&T Clark, 1968.

Schreiner, Thomas R. "Penal Substitution View." In *The Nature of the Atonement: Four Views*, edited by James K. Beilby and Paul Rhodes Eddy, 67–98. Downers Grove: IVP Academic, 2006.

Sherman, Robert. *King, Priest and Prophet: A Trinitarian Theology of Atonement*. New York: T&T Clark, 2004.

Sophocles. *Sophocles I: Antigone, Oedipus the King, Oedipus at Colonus*. Translated by David Grene. Chicago: University of Chicago Press, 1991.

Spjuth, Roland. "Gustaf Aulén." In *Bloomsbury Companion to the Atonement*, edited by Adam J. Johnson. New York: Bloomsbury, forthcoming.

Strobel, Kyle. *Jonathan Edwards's Theology: A Reinterpretation*. New York: T&T Clark, 2013.

Sykes, Stephen. *The Story of Atonement*. London: Darton, Longman, and Todd, 1997.

Thomas Aquinas. *Prologue to Aquinas's Commentary on the Sentences*. Translated by Ralph McInerny. Dominican House of Studies – Priory of the Immaculate Conception. Accessed April 20, 2016. http://dhspriory.org/thomas/english/Sentences.htm.

―――. *Light of Faith: The Compendium of Theology*. Manchester, NH: Sophia Institute Press, 1993.

―――. *Selected Writings*. Translated by Ralph McInerny. New York: Penguin, 1998.

―――. *Summa Theologica*. Translated by Fathers of the English Dominican Province. Westminster: Christian Classics, 1981.

Timpe, Kevin, and Craig A. Boyd. *Virtues and Their Vices*. New York: Oxford University Press, 2014.

Tolkien, J. R. R. *The Lord of the Rings*. Boston: Houghton Mifflin, 2004.

Torrance, Thomas F. *Atonement: The Person and Work of Christ*. Downers Grove, IL: InterVarsity Press, 2009.

―――. *The Mediation of Christ*. Colorado Springs: Helmers & Howard, 1992.

Treat, Jeremy R. *The Crucified King: Atonement and Kingdom in Biblical and Systematic Theology*. Grand Rapids: Zondervan, 2014.

Treier, Daniel J. *Proverbs & Ecclesiastes*. Brazos Theological Commentary. Grand Rapids: Brazos, 2011.

―――. "Wisdom." In *Dictionary for Theological Interpretation of the Bible*, edited by Kevin J. Vanhoozer, Craig G. Bartholomew,

Daniel J. Treier, and N. T. Wright, 844–47. Grand Rapids: Baker Academic, 2005.

Vanhoozer, Kevin J. *The Drama of Doctrine: A Canonical-Linguistic Approach to Christian Theology*. Louisville: Westminster John Knox, 2005.

Waltke, Bruce K., with Charles Yu. *An Old Testament Theology: An Exegetical, Canonical, and Thematic Approach*. Grand Rapids: Zondervan, 2007.

Wood, W. Jay. "Prudence." In *Virtues and Their Vices*, edited by Kevin Timpe and Craig A. Boyd, 37–58. New York: Oxford University Press, 2014.

Wright, N. T. *Paul and the Faithfulness of God*. Minneapolis: Fortress, 2013.

SUBJECT AND AUTHOR INDEX

SCRIPTURE INDEX

Old Testament